Praise for Make It Work

"A must-read for anyone who wants to make the most of his or her career. The grass is not always greener on the other side, and this book can help leverage an individual's existing career."
—Cile Johnson, senior manager, Creative Leadership Council,
Center for Creative Leadership

"I finally got the courage to let everyone in the organization know my plan. Make It Work *gave me clear direction on how to achieve my goal, especially how to get people I thought would be difficult to become champions of my plan. It is a confidence builder!"*
—Katherine Duncan, executive director,
Moulin Rouge Museum & Cultural Center, Inc.

"A breath of fresh air in challenging the conventional wisdom about career success, this is a book worth reading. Two thumbs up for Make It Work!*"*
—Joseph R. Weintraub and James M. Hunt, professors of management,
Babson College; coauthors, The Coaching Manager

"A must for anyone searching for job fulfillment and success in their current organization. It is loaded with practical exercises designed to help you discover your passionate core, craft your ideal job, and navigate your organization to make it happen. Read Make It Work, *do the exercises, and start enjoying true success today!"*
—Don P. Martone, founder & president, Martone Limited LLC

"Celebrates the organization and advocates for the individual in that organization. Make It Work provides the GPS (global positioning system) for an individual dealing with the dynamic, fluid nature of organizational career life today."

—Victoria A. Guthrie, senior fellow,
Innovative Program Initiatives, Center for Creative Leadership

"A win-win strategy that's real! This professional philosophy has the potential to change the landscape of business and volunteer organizations everywhere."

—RaeAnn L. Osborne, professor, Montgomery College;
president, Children's Volunteer Organization, LDS Church

"I had become totally dissatisfied with the performance of a once top-performing manager. Using the tools in Make It Work, together we determined his level of frustration and immediately got him back on track—driving the train!"

—Bart K. Maybie, president, CBC Financial Corporation

"Not only a great book for those who want to find more job satisfaction without leaving their organization, but an excellent resource for anyone wanting to create a more meaningful experience in any professional setting. This book could go a long way toward helping individuals create not only a better job, but even a better life."

—Bill Crawford, founder & president, Crawford Performance Solutions

"Frodsham and Gargiulo are refreshing! Their hopeful message and the practical tools they provide allow readers to remain in their organization while reshaping their role with passion and 'the heart.' Terrific new thinking."

—Michael P. Tobin, Ph.D., MICA Consulting Partners

"Supplies universal and powerful principles to forward-looking people who want to experience greater control over their lives. The book focuses us, clearly and directly, on what can be done to take charge of our work environment. It is inspiring and insightful in finding individual and organizational success."

—Chris DeVault, gobal recruiting manager,
Goodman Manufacturing Co., L.P.

"**Make It Work** *is the long overdue career conversation that each of us seeking greater professional fulfillment should have with ourself. You won't find a more up-to-date and practical guide for achieving true career wealth in today's demanding business environment.*"

—*Sean Rohen, Mentoring Systems Consultants*

"**Make It Work** *has many problem-solving and decision-making techniques that can help you in everyday challenges, even if you don't have a job.*"

—*Stephen Rybar, former FBI*

"*Stop playing the games, stop being what you think they want. This book will lead you through a process of discovery about yourself that will unleash the energizing power of passion.*"

—*Wm. Bruce Rea, P.Eng., MBA, former senior executive, high school teacher*

Make It Work

Make
It
Work

Navigate Your Career Without Leaving Your Organization

JOE FRODSHAM AND **BILL GARGIULO**

Davies-Black Publishing
Mountain View, California

Published by Davies-Black Publishing, a division of CPP, Inc., 1055 Joaquin Road, Suite 200, Mountain View, CA 94043; 800-624-1765.

Special discounts on bulk quantities of Davies-Black books are available to corporations, professional associations, and other organizations. For details, contact the Director of Marketing and Sales at Davies-Black Publishing; 650-691-9123; fax 650-623-9271.

Visit the Davies-Black Publishing Web site at www.daviesblack.com.

09 08 07 06 05 10 9 8 7 6 5 4 3 2 1
Printed in the United States of America

Library of Congress Cataloging-in-Publication Data
Frodsham, Joe
    Make it work: navigate your career without leaving your organization / Joe Frodsham and Bill Gargiulo— 1st ed.
        p. cm.
Includes index.
    ISBN 0-89106-208-4 (pbk.)
    1. Career development. I. Gargiulo, Bill. II. Title.
HF5381.F7755 2005
650.1—dc22

                                                                        2005000516

FIRST EDITION
First printing 2005

To my eternal partner and wife, Kris Frodsham, and the four children who bring me endless joy, Sydney, Tate, Kennedy, and Davis. Your patience with husband and dad is much appreciated . . . and needed.
—Joe Frodsham

To my daughter, Rachael, who has inspired me to love and reach for what is highest within myself, and to my mother and father, who have always supported my growth and passions—thank you.
—Bill Gargiulo

Contents

Introduction

The mass of men lead lives of quiet desperation.
—*Henry David Thoreau*

Through our years of helping leaders and professionals develop, we have repeatedly confirmed the following fact: Most adults feel they are in the midst of a mediocre career in their organization. We find that disturbing. As adults, we spend the biggest part of our lives working in organizations, so a mediocre career often translates into a mediocre life, an existence that is just okay with some ups and some downs. And unfortunately, those who want a better-than-mediocre career and life are often frustrated as they work hard and follow the common career advice but still experience little career mobility and a chronic sense of dissatisfaction. When their efforts don't bear fruit they give up hoping and trying, and start treating their job as a "nine-to-five necessity." And maybe they start looking for another "better" job in another "better" organization.

In looking for greener pastures to build a career, you are probably assuming that the problems with your current career are caused by your circumstances—the bad leadership, problems, and lack of opportunities in your current organization. Based on this assumption, you invest the time to find and move into another organization, often expending significant effort and even money in learning to navigate your new company, reestablish your credibility and networks, and move your loved ones to unfamiliar geographies. And along with the numerous tangible and intangible costs of moving to a new company comes risk! Most of the time the greener pastures you left for are not so green after all. In fact, a few months into the new job and company you will probably find that the career issues you were leaving in your previous company will start reemerging. This is because in your zest to improve your career you focused your efforts on changing where you work instead of staying and aligning with the truths of career success.

The career-related patterns and issues in which you constantly find yourself are not a result of the problems in your company. They are largely a result of the way you think and act. Trying to improve your career success by simply finding a new place to work is like trying to run faster by finding a new track to run on. Your career success will come from adopting the beliefs and behaviors that drive career success in every organization you choose to be in.

If you keep doing what you've been doing, you will keep getting what you've got. The same career beliefs and behaviors will get you the same results in every organization in which you choose to work. Achieving career success begins with a clear understanding that you don't need to, and probably shouldn't, leave your current organization. Instead of wasting your time finding and transitioning into a new role, invest that time in adopting the principles and practices of what we call "career wealth." *Make It Work* is dedicated to helping you find passion and success within your organization. So don't return the headhunter calls, stop updating your resume, and invest this time in learning and navigating the path to career wealth in your current organization. This path starts with your heart.

Your Heart + Your Organization = Your Success

As authors, we view the subject of careers and career transformation both personally and professionally. Personally in that like you we have at times struggled to find career fulfillment and financial reward within the companies where we have worked. And professionally in that our personal career transformation has put us in leadership roles building people and talent systems in organizations. Over the past two years we have spent thousands of hours using our unique perch in organizations to test and refine the principles of career transformation and success. The principles we have developed are universal and powerful. And they find their source in the same place—the heart. Quite simply, your career fulfillment is not to be found in the latest career success books, tapes, or "systems." Instead, the answer is in you, or more specifically in what you love. We want you to be aware of this fact: The people who achieve sustained fulfillment in their career are those who have made a choice to do what they love.

W. H. Murray, in *The Story of Everest* (1953), says, "Concerning all acts of initiative and creation, there is one elementary truth— that the moment one definitely commits oneself, then providence moves too." When you make that deep, heartfelt commitment, it generates opportunities through both predictable and unpredictable—even amazing—ways. Although simple and intuitive, this act of effectively bringing what you love into your work and life is not always easy and, in fact, is quite rare.

Looking for Love in All the Wrong Places

Broadly speaking, we all want the same thing: a great job doing what we love to do and being supported, that is, recognized and rewarded for it. So, if we all want it, why is it so elusive? Why do most of us find career success at times but often feel we have to make trade-offs, even give up some of what we want and love to do to survive and get ahead in our organization? Why do we feel we have to leave our organization as if we were trapped? It points to a pervasive sense of career unrest that is largely the result of two consistent facts:

1. The companies and organizations we work in are not in the business of considering and aligning with our loves and passions. Instead, they often separate us from what we love and even need, causing us to conform to what people in the organization want from us. This happens subtly. When we're in an organization, as in any social situation, our inherent response is to do what is necessary to fit in and get along with others, especially those in authority. In doing so, we often give up what we love and need and become a slave to this impersonal thing called "the company."

2. Much of the widely accepted career advice is false and even toxic. By following the conventional precepts, people are actually ensuring that they won't achieve sustained career fulfillment and wealth. In the context of history, modern organizations are relatively new—you are probably no more than three generations removed from ancestors who either worked on a small farm or had a career within a smaller family-owned business. Perhaps because of this we are still in the corporate dark ages, collectively struggling to understand how organizations really work and how more people can find success and fulfillment within them.

As authors—and now as coauthors—we have looked at careers and career wealth with a critical eye. We have seen what works and what does not work. We have identified the misunderstood, even counterintuitive, principles that drive real career success. The principles that help people effectively bring their loves to work are the guideposts for those few people in organizations who continually realize sustained career success and fulfillment. Because many of these principles directly contradict conventional wisdom about careers, they go unnoticed by the vast majority of people. Instead, tens of millions continue the career/company grind, never fully realizing love, passion, and fulfillment, and they don't know what to do about it.

For coauthor Joe Frodsham, the static nature of common career thinking came into clearer focus earlier in his career. While leading a group of professionals within a large multinational technology company, he met with a program coordinator on his staff to discuss her performance and development plan for the coming year. As a normal part of this conversation, they discussed her longer-term career aspirations, during which time she shared her career anguish. She did not feel challenged by her work but felt she had no chance to move up in the company because she had not earned a college degree; and as a single mother, she felt she did not have the time or resources to pursue that course.

When Joe asked her what kind of work she enjoyed and what she would like to study, she seemed unsure. After further discussion, it became apparent that her basic belief was that career satisfaction would come almost solely from being promoted. The substance and nature of her work didn't matter; it was the title and money that would signify to her and others that she had arrived and was fulfilled. In further conversations with members of his staff, Joe found that they were in about the same place—wanting and waiting for promotions to achieve career fulfillment. This was the attraction—the promise of promotion—for which they were willing to move to new organizations and even geographies.

This experience inspired both of us to take an intensive look at the relationship between doing what we love and achieving career wealth. Over the past two years we have both spent thousands of hours answering questions such as

- Is it possible to do what we love and still get ahead in an organization?

- What can we learn from the relatively few who consistently achieve career wealth?

- Why are job fulfillment and success within an organization so elusive?

For the knowledge and wisdom gained through this research, we thank the program coordinator who began this quest. And if we could have that same career discussion again, we would tell her the answer to her career anguish does not lie in a college degree or an elevated title or a higher salary. Those are not bad things, but her ability to achieve these symbols of success would increase exponentially when she first dedicated herself to doing what she loves. The rest of the practices of career wealth can be learned and coached.

As we have assisted those willing to transform their careers, we have solidified our principles. We have also had the time of our lives as we have been doing what we love. Indeed, uncovering these career principles and truths and helping people transform their career within their organization is our love and passion. And it is with this passion that we share *Make It Work* with you.

Stay in Your Organization and Succeed

The first chapter introduces the fundamental role of love and passion in realizing sustained success in your organization and in your life. You will assess your current level of career success by completing a short self-assessment called the Career Wealth Indicator. This self-awareness exercise will help provide the basis from which you will begin to build your career. We then begin to establish the fundamental beliefs that set the basis for all successful careers by exposing the pervasive career myths that limit your career opportunities. We focus on helping you to understand and adopt the critical career truths that will put you on the higher path to career wealth. Throughout the rest of the book, you will then move sequentially through the career-building process.

Part 1, "Your Career Foundation," will lead you through the four steps for establishing your career foundation. At the core of the four-step process is your heart—encompassing the things you actually need in your work to find passion and wealth in your company and career. In this process, you will uncover your unique passions and the needs they fulfill for you, and you will identify and declare the career direction you will take in your organization. The career foundation steps involve significant introspection through the use of Discovery Exercises. Once you have completed them you will have the awareness, energy, and direction needed to effectively shape your career in your organization regardless of your reputation, history, or circumstances.

Part 2, "Your Career Navigation," will help you to adopt six practices for effectively working in an organization. As with the process for establishing your career foundation, each of these powerful practices is supported by a Discovery Exercise. Learning these practices will enable you to shape your perfect role and have your organization support and reward you for doing so. Ultimately, you will realize career success while adding substantially more value to your organization.

Make It Work has been designed to help you transform your career within the organization you have chosen. So get ready for your own transformation. It's absolutely worth the effort.

Let's get started!

About the Authors

Joe Frodsham has had a successful career as an employee and leader in organizations. He has worked with some of the most successful companies in the world and has led groups and change initiatives in companies such as Compaq Computer Corporation, Anderson Consulting, and Whirlpool Corporation. He is seen as a thought leader on leadership and organization development, is a sought-after speaker, and has published articles on internal consulting and development.

Frodsham loves helping people and organizations align with the real principles that drive success and wealth. Since making his love his life's work, he has helped many people find sustained success within a company. His approach and insights are unique and often revealing, cutting through the jargon and fluff that pervade literature on careers, companies, and success. He gets to the core truths and then makes them practical and applicable.

Originally from western Canada, Frodsham received both a bachelor's degree and a master's degree in organizational behavior from Brigham Young University. He currently resides in Michigan with his wife, Kris, and their four children. To contact him, please visit www.careerswork.com.

Bill Gargiulo is passionate about working with people, helping them discover what they love to do and then find a way to do it within the context of an organization. His primary focus in organizations has been on talent management, leadership development, performance management and employee engagement, and organizational effectiveness and culture change.

A true multicultural leader, Gargiulo speaks several languages and draws insight from a childhood spent on five continents. He holds an undergraduate degree in liberal arts from Denison University and a Graduate International MBA degree from Thunderbird University. He lives in Michigan and enjoys writing and traveling.

Don't Leave
Your
Organization

---

*I never came upon any of my discoveries through
the process of rational thinking.*
—*Albert Einstein*

One of the most pervasive phenomena of our modern age is the rise and influence of *organizations* in our lives. Prior to the industrial age most people were relatively self-sufficient, with the only true organizations being the church and the state. Outside these entities people looked to family, friends, and neighbors for support, employment, education, and exchange of goods.

The Current Role of Organizations

Over the past hundred years all of this has changed. Now we have replaced reliance on family and community with a heavy reliance on formal organizations and companies. From an early age we are educated and even parented by formal institutions. As we get

1

older, we find employment within companies, and often our extracurricular activities are supported by formal organizations such as clubs, associations, and churches.

The rise and influence of organizations in our lives has led to some profound changes in our society. The role of our local neighborhood has diminished as people now find friendship, employment, education, and meaning in the workplace. Many of us never meet our neighbors yet build strong relationships with our co-workers, and the pull of our neighborhood rarely keeps us from moving if we find the right position elsewhere.

Realizing the huge role organizations play in our lives leads to one obvious yet critical conclusion: Your life success and fulfillment are largely determined by your ability to bring yourself and what you love into your organization. As such, it's in your self-interest to learn to navigate effectively the companies and organizations you choose to be part of.

For many of us, navigating, or "getting ahead," in a company is difficult. Sometimes company decisions that impact our job and career don't make sense or appear to be unfair. Other times we are not sure what we really want. Unfortunately, there is a lot of bad advice in the world, and following the path prescribed by the company or outside experts can actually lead to more frustration than progress. Constantly we work with people who feel stuck in their career—after years of doing all the right things they still aren't really fulfilled.

Each company is different yet fundamentally the same. The same in that every company is made up of people with similar needs, agendas, and thus predictable patterns of behavior. Understanding these basic principles and patterns gives us insight and power, enabling us to proactively navigate the social and political realities in our company.

It is easy to blame a sense of career dissatisfaction on our organization and/or its leaders and focus on them in our attempts to get ahead in our career. Many people spend much of their precious time trying to shape and influence the way others in their organization see them. They do this under the false belief that "getting in good" with the boss will bring them career fulfillment. At best, this focus on people and politics brings periodic security;

however, it never brings a sustained sense of career passion and success. This comes only by looking inside oneself and understanding the matters of one's heart. Artist Marc Chagall said, "If I create from the heart, nearly everything works, if from the head, almost nothing." Whether you are a graphic designer or a human resources assistant, the root of your career success lies in what you love.

Let's look at your true motivations.

The Source of Career Energy and Wealth

Societies flourish when they harness energy sources. Just as the Hoover Dam provides the electricity to light up Las Vegas, and the dams along the Yellow River provide the electricity to fuel a modern Shanghai, those things you love generate energy and power for your career. When your loves don't find expression in your career, it's like trying to draw electricity from a rock. You and your spirit are dulled and you are left to go through the motions and grab at the symbols of success—money and titles—without fuel for true career fulfillment and success.

Alignment with your loves is so powerful and pervasive that it affects every aspect of your career and life. When you don't love your work, it negatively impacts your physical, mental, and emotional health and the quality of relationships you build with others. Trying to improve your career by focusing on the emotional and physical symptoms will only put a band-aid on a festering wound. This is why your career transformation begins by going to the source, your heart.

A number of behaviors and feelings clearly indicate the level of alignment a person has with what he or she loves. Many of these behaviors and feelings are assessed in Discovery Exercise 1, "Career Wealth Indicator."

Within any organization your job, manager, and work will change. As they change, often so does the level of alignment with your heart. That's why for most people a sense of career fulfillment is in flux. Sometimes we are fulfilled in our work and

DISCOVERY EXERCISE 1
Career Wealth Indicator

Directions: Assess each of the twenty-five pairs of statements in each row below on a scale of 0–2. Circle the number that most closely indicates your assessment. Interpret your results at the end of the exercise.

Scale: 0 = The statement on the left is currently true
1 = Both statements are somewhat true
2 = The statement on the right is currently true

I hate to get up and go to work every morning.	0 (1) 2	I love to get up and go to work every morning.
I can never just be myself at work.	0 1 2	I can always be myself at work.
I always worry about what people think when I share my opinions.	0 1 2	I can express myself regardless of what others think.
I rarely feel well physically (I get colds, headaches, etc.).	0 1 2	I enjoy really good health and rarely feel hampered physically.
If I could escape, I would.	0 1 2	If I had total financial freedom, I would still do the work I am doing.
I am not learning anything new on my job.	0 1 2	I am constantly learning something new; I am becoming more capable.
I never catch a break where I work.	0 1 2	There is an abundance of opportunities; I don't have time to chase them all.

I feel sad at work.	0 1 2	I feel energized and challenged by my work, and I am happy with it.
I do not enjoy being with my co-workers.	0 1 2	I am energized by my co-workers.
The paycheck keeps me doing my job.	0 1 2	I would do this work for no pay.
I find myself constantly wishing I were somewhere else.	0 1 2	I'm right where I want to be.
I spend all my time doing work I do not enjoy.	0 1 2	I spend all my time doing work I truly love to do.
I wait for the company to tell me what they will do with me.	0 1 2	I create my own opportunities.
My job confines me.	0 1 2	My work enlightens me.
My work is a "nine-to-five necessity."	0 1 2	My work is a key part of who I am.
I always focus on what others think about me and adjust to it.	0 1 2	I never worry about what others think about me and my work—I am my own audience.
I live for my weekends and vacations.	0 1 2	I find my work as enjoyable as a vacation; I don't need a break.
I don't dare share my ambitions and loves—What's the use?	0 1 2	Others may underestimate me—I don't care.

DISCOVERY EXERCISE 1 CONT'D

I spend my time doing what I am told to do.	0	1	2	I spend my time doing what I choose to do.
I react and respond.	0	1	2	I create.
I find myself exhausted before I go home.	0	1	2	I gain energy during the day from the work I am doing.
I regularly complain about my job.	0	1	2	I regularly tell people about the great things I am working on.
I am always overlooked on my job.	0	1	2	People and opportunities are attracted to me.
I spend my time doing what others want me to do, not doing what I love.	0	1	2	I spend my time doing what I love, not what others want me to do.
Someday I'll get to do more of what I love to do.	0	1	2	I insist on doing what I love every day.

Add up the numbers you circled and record the total below.

Career Wealth Indicator Score _____

Interpretation: Your score is somewhere between 0 and 50. As you've probably guessed, the higher your score, the more your loves are currently finding expression in your work and career.

  0–20 = You are feeling the effects of a job that is mostly to totally misaligned with those things you love

21–40 = You are experiencing some ups and some downs, indicating that there are aspects of your work that ignite the energy of your loves

41–50 = You are in a role in which you are generally doing what you love

sometimes we are not. Whatever your Career Wealth Indicator score, the challenge is to uncover what you love and bring that effectively into your work and career. Doing so will ensure that your career wealth is not left to happenstance. It will allow you to take fuller control of your career and life happiness. The rest of this book is dedicated to helping you do that. We will begin by exposing the predominant career myths and the less-known career truths that establish the enlightened and empowered path to career wealth.

Uncovering
Career Myths
and Truths

When you started in the full-time work world, you were likely full of rational yet possibly incorrect beliefs concerning how to be successful and happy in your work and career. In fact, at this point you are probably still holding on to many inaccurate career assumptions such as the popular belief that if you work hard, the organization will take care of you. We are sorry to say this belief and many like it are rarely correct. Holding on to them is bound to result in periodic disillusionment and even despair as your faulty assumptions keep you needlessly shackled to a continuous cycle of heightened expectations and letdowns. Many people adapt to this cycle of frustration by throwing up their hands and giving up many of their career aspirations. This common response then sets in motion a career of mediocrity.

The fact that virtually everyone starts and continues in their career with faulty beliefs should not be surprising. There are no formal courses on how to be successful in a real organization. It is not taught in our high school or college curriculum, and the advice we receive from managers and mentors is often toxic, as it is based on faulty assumptions and clichés, things that they may believe to be true but often do not lead to a successful and happy career. It is little wonder that most people stop trying to find fulfillment within their work in an organization as career success seems to make no sense and to be out of their control.

Enabling beliefs are the base foundation of your career wealth. As with a cracked or not fully set foundation of a house, everything built upon it will eventually fall. So, your path to career wealth begins with learning and adopting helpful and accurate career assumptions.

Based on our experience we have identified sixteen faulty assumptions, many of which are widely accepted, and any one of which can lead to behaviors that will limit and even derail a career. We call these career-limiting beliefs *career myths*. Accompanying each career myth is a corresponding foundational truth. Reviewing and adopting these foundational truths is invaluable to establishing effective career behaviors and realizing career wealth.

Before reviewing this list of career myths and truths, check your current career beliefs by completing Discovery Exercise 2.

DISCOVERY EXERCISE 2
Your Career Beliefs

List below your career assumptions, specifically the five to ten most important things people must think or do to achieve career wealth (fulfillment and success) throughout their career.

1.

2.

3.

4.

5.

6.

7.

8.

9.

10.

Career Myths and Career Truths

People and organizations are full of accepted beliefs and assumptions. However, widespread acceptance doesn't make something true. Until the fifteenth century almost everyone believed the earth was flat. Like this old belief concerning the shape of the earth, many of the widely accepted career beliefs are really nothing more than myths. They keep us stuck, unable to explore and reach our promised land.

Many of the sixteen career myths described below are accepted beliefs and practices for finding career wealth; however, they often can have the real effect of distancing you from your career success. You will find that many of the career truths contradict accepted practices for attaining career wealth, which may explain why so many people experience career frustration. As you read each one, compare it to your list of career assumptions in Discovery Exercise 2 and consider the degree to which you have managed your career based on myth or truth.

MYTH #1
You must manage your image—be your own brand.

This approach to career success has been present for quite some time and currently seems to be experiencing a resurgence. It postulates that career success comes from managing your image, spending your time shaping certain impressions of yourself in the minds of others—in other words, focusing your energies on *style* instead of *substance*.

With the "be your own brand" approach, rather than spending your time and energy creating and shaping what most matters to you, you are spending your time and energy determining whether your actions and behaviors fit with how you want to be seen and perceived. In this scenario you are in a prison of your own making, always worrying about what others are thinking and whether their perceptions are what you want them to be.

(cont'd)

This myth has pervaded almost all the literature on career success. Whether it's some best-selling book like *Dress for Success* or the myriad of career seminars offered throughout the world, they are all built on the premise that managing outer appearances will promote your success. However, as you study those who have really achieved sustained career wealth, you will find that they represent every different look, style, and demeanor. Their success didn't come from emulating others or maintaining an image. Instead, it came from being themselves and being dedicated to working on things they love.

This is so critical. People feel great anxiety when their real loves and feelings don't find expression in their work. So many feel they have to put on a mask and behave in ways they think others will approve of. But behind the mask, it's clear their work is full of drudgery. Every aspect of their life is affected—mind, body, spirit, and relationships. For many, it takes a crisis or a time of introspection for them to decide to take off the mask and be themselves. When they make this decision, they liberate themselves and find that people respond better to the real person.

Clearly, being your own brand is a waste of time and will actually derail your path to career wealth. Instead of managing your image, you should be clear on who you are and what you love, and find opportunities to pursue this within your organization. We all love to watch and be around people who are passionate about what they do. Whether it is the musician, athlete, leader, or accountant who is doing what he or she loves, we can't help but watch and admire them. Each of us can do the same if we take off our mask and find the work we are most passionate about.

This is the first and most important truth behind career wealth—everything else rests upon it!

* * *

TRUTH #1
You must be yourself and do what you love!

MYTH #2
The company will take care of you.

At a fundamental level there is no such thing as a company. It is not a tangible thing, but instead a construct used to describe a group of people working, hopefully, toward a common purpose as it aligns with their self-interest. When managing your career you should be careful not to think of a company or organization as a person or entity that has any obligation to take care of or develop you. In fact, it is unlikely that any person or manager in your company will go out of his or her way to ensure that all your personal and career needs are taken care of.

With the downsizing, cost cutting, and corporate greed of the last decade you would think people would know better than to hand their full trust to any one organization. Apparently many of us still want to believe in the dated notion of a paternalistic company that owes us something, and as a result we abdicate important decisions. The fact is that entitlement is dying! If you put your full trust in a company, you surrender your power and leave yourself open to ultimate disappointment. The bottom line is that career wealth comes from relying on yourself, not on your company. Instead of spending your time asking and waiting for the company to give you what you want, you should focus on answering the following questions:

- How can I do what I love inside my organization?

- How can I keep my opportunities and options open inside and outside my company?

* * *

TRUTH #2
You are your own company—take care of yourself.

MYTH #3
To get ahead, you just need to do a good job.

We all want this to be true. It would seem to make sense that the quality and integrity of a person's work are all that should matter. Unfortunately, getting ahead in an organization often takes more than that. To be clear, maintaining a high level of performance is critical; however, doing a good job does not guarantee you will get ahead or find career wealth in your company. Ultimately, organizations are political, and personnel and promotion decisions are based on rational performance criteria and nonrational subjective criteria. So, doing a good job is necessary but not sufficient. You also need to effectively navigate the social and political dimensions of your company.

Although politics are always present, they should not be the primary focus of your attention. Nor should they solely shape your decisions and actions within an organization. The real power comes from navigating the politics but not being political. Your main focus should be on doing what you love, not on being accepted and included by all the "important" people. Being a political animal will ensure that you are not bringing your loves to work, but instead relying on the transient affection of your coworkers.

*   *   *

TRUTH #3
Politics are inevitable—you must learn how to navigate them.

MYTH #4
It is important to have work/life balance.

This is a myth that has been in vogue for over a decade. Company surveys, HR departments, and numerous training vendors have focused on measuring and promoting a healthy balance between employee life inside and outside of work. Although this myth is well intentioned, it's based on a dated assumption that one's "work" and "life" are separate and that a certain number of work hours are in the realm of acceptability—while too much or too little time dedicated to your work life is unhealthy. This treats work as something arduous, a set of tasks the company expects in return for money and rewards. In this assumption, people put in their time and then get on with their real life.

This separation between work and life is a relatively new phenomenon. It started in the twentieth century as the majority of people found employment in organizations away from the shop or fields around their home. In moving to an organizational setting to work, we have lost an important understanding: Our work is a key part of our lives. And, since everybody's life is not the same, neither should the time they dedicate to their work. In other words, balance means different things to different people and, if people are working at what they love, it is not "work" they are doing. They simply look at it as their life. So instead of focusing on the time people spend "working" and "living," the real aim should be to ensure that people's work lives are aligned with their passions; that is, that they are living while they are working.

* * *

TRUTH #4
It's not about work/life balance;
it's about finding your life's work.

MYTH #5
Company decisions are made rationally.

Yours would be a sterile, unprogressive company if all decisions were based on rational analysis. Companies are made up of people, and people are innately political, non-rational, and complex. There is great freedom in not judging and critiquing the "silly" decisions made in your company but instead accepting the wide variety of perspectives as an acceptable and interesting part of working with others. To achieve career wealth, you need to move from being a critical bystander to being someone who accepts and effectively works within the political realities of your organization.

* * *

TRUTH #5
Both rational and nonrational thinking are always present and necessary.

MYTH #6
You will get ahead by doing what key managers in your organization want (the "yes-person" syndrome).

The logic is clear, since key managers have the ability to reward and punish. If you do what they say and keep them happy, you will have more rewards and "get ahead." Although this logic is clear, it rarely works that way. By doing everything you are asked and asking no questions, you reinforce a belief that you are less capable than those who give the orders. It can also lead to inferior decisions, as managers are not given the alternative perspectives they need to refine ideas.

Being a yes-person will endear you to others, and often provides a safe and level career path to slowly and cautiously walk on; however, this is not a way to align to your passions and create what matters to you most. Once you identify and declare your career passions, it may or may not be on people's agenda to support you. In fact, in the short term declaring your passions and pushing back may create some discomfort; however, in one way or another your environment will align with you, creating a launching pad from which you can't help but "get ahead."

* * *

TRUTH #6
Being a yes-person will limit and frustrate you in your career.

MYTH #7
Career paths are predictable.

Just like people, career paths can be either predictable or unpredictable. They can be rational or emotional. Your career path need not be confined to the predictable parameters and actions defined by an organization. At any moment, you can shape your career in both conventional and unconventional ways if you so choose. In fact, a mark of those who have achieved sustained career wealth is having traveled a different road than most—one aligned with their passions, not common conventions. It's not a coincidence that many of the truly successful high-tech leaders did not finish college. They had the courage to step away from a predictable career path and follow their passions.

It's clear that many people either don't trust their passions or don't know what they are passionate about. In working with people engaged in making career decisions, we have often seen them resort to the safe path, feeling that they need to get a traditional degree in business or law to ensure career employment and

(cont'd)

progression. There is nothing inherently wrong with a traditional path unless it is not aligned to what you really want to do. Those who find career wealth know there is enough room in the world markets to make a terrific living doing what they love. Whether it is math, fly-fishing, or urban sociology, there are ways of building a fruitful career around it. Career wealth begins with clear alignment with your passions. Once aligned, you may or may not follow a traditional career path.

*   *   *

TRUTH #7
There may not be a traditional career path that aligns with your passions—don't let that stop you.

MYTH #8
Career progression requires a formal career path.

At one point in your career you may have developed, or been given, a career plan. In fact, the promise of a formal career path often attracts people to organizations. In such a planned path, the set of jobs and experiences outlined over an extended period—five to ten years, for example—brings a sense of predictability and comfort, giving people a false sense that their career will take a certain course.

In reality, organizations and careers are necessarily much more fluid. Markets, strategies, and organizational structures always change over time, in the process changing the types of roles offered in a company, surfacing opportunities that previously were not available or even considered. This is especially true in the dynamic times we live in. With globalization, restructuring, acquisitions, and downsizing being the norm, there is little predictability in careers. Time and again we've seen opportunities emerge that could never have been predicted. So, instead of developing a formal career path, the strategy should be to learn all you can while in your current role and always be open to opportunities that allow you to do what you love. Call it career improvisation.

Career improvisation does not mean you don't have career direction or a sense of the type of roles you want to assume as you progress through your career. Instead, it suggests that you are open to opportunities and not constrained to a defined path. One thing is for sure—your career will not be a straight road, but instead will be full of twists and hills. So, be ready for the ride and get ready to turn and change gears.

* * *

TRUTH #8
You can't fully plan a great career—
so be ready to improvise.

MYTH #9
Once stuck or stereotyped within an organization,
there is nothing you can do about it.

If you believe this, it will become a self-fulfilling prophecy. However, if you believe your past does not have to dictate your present or future, then you will find a new locus of power and influence. Perceptions of others are a transient thing; they are constantly changing based on momentary issues and contingencies. Ironically, if your focus is on changing others' perceptions of you, you will probably be unsuccessful. It is never too late to change your beliefs and reenergize your career, but it starts by letting go of others' perceptions and caring more fully about doing the work you are passionate about.

* * *

TRUTH #9
You must focus on the work,
not others' perceptions of you.

MYTH #10
You need to find a career doing what you are good at.

This myth sets the premise for almost all traditional career counseling and promotional decision making. The simple idea is that if you do work that you are good at, you will find greater prosperity and stability in your career. Additionally, companies benefit too, as you are providing maximum value to them.

Based on this, schools and companies administer standard aptitude tests, report cards, and various evaluation processes focused on driving awareness and alignment with a person's measured strengths. And, when making career and promotional decisions, the level, function, and role a person is placed in are based on how others in the organization assess his or her capabilities. Other factors such as a person's interests are rarely considered. It is simply a given that we are to organize our passions, perspectives, and lives around the needs of the organization.

Clearly, it is always a good idea to be aware of your areas of strength and weaknesses. However, when your areas of perceived aptitude are the primary reason for choosing and following a career direction, you run the risk of not tapping into the real source of career wealth—your passions.

Techniques for evaluating your capabilities are often faulty and inaccurate. Time and again we've seen people who were told not to pursue a career direction because they weren't smart enough or "inclined" in a certain area. Years later they regained the confidence and awareness that they *did* have the capability. Unfortunately, by the time they stopped listening to "experts," they had spent years in less fulfilling careers doing what they were "good at."

What's clear is that people's talents and abilities aren't always the same as their passions. As authors we have regularly received feedback that we are good at managing, developing presentations, and leading conferences. In fact we have constantly been given this kind of work because we are good at it, but we are not passionate about this work. Finding our own career wealth and fulfillment began with stopping the grind (doing things we were talented in but hated) and embracing the work we love to do.

We believe the coming years will bring an emerging awareness of the need for passion in the workplace. People in companies will see that tapping into the passions, not necessarily the overt strengths, of people will spark higher levels of sustained effort and results.

* * *

TRUTH #10
You must find a career doing what you love.

MYTH #11
Rocking the boat will sink your career.

It is every person's right and desire to create, shape, build, develop, grow, and achieve career wealth. If this rocks the boat once in a while, then so be it. Few people actually achieve career wealth. Instead of stepping out and doing what they love, they try to fit in and get along, many times deferring and repressing their opinions, interests, and passions because they may be seen as different or controversial. Sure, it is nice to work well with people, but when it comes at the price of forgoing doing what you love, the price is too high.

Achieving career wealth at times takes courage as it may require you to rock the boat in productive ways. Often it's not what you say but how you say it. As you work through the Career Wealth Model (see pp. 27–29), you will build the passion, confidence, and organizational savvy to rock the boat in productive ways.

* * *

TRUTH #11
If the boat is rocking, you might as well try to enjoy the ride.

MYTH #12
Someone will tell you if you are performing poorly or do not have a future with the company.

Although it would be ideal if your manager were open and transparent with you, this rarely happens. Most managers feel very uncomfortable about providing open and honest feedback. As a result, you can spend years unaware of the opinions that your manager and other key stakeholders have of you.

At a basic level, learning and development cannot occur without feedback. Simply put, people can't learn and adjust without understanding how they affect others. Given the importance of feedback to your learning and development, you need to surmount any aversion you have toward soliciting open and transparent feedback and start asking for it.

Indeed, if you are not receiving regular feedback, do not assume you are in great standing. In fact, you may have some blind spots—negative perceptions that you are unaware of that, if they continue, will limit your career options. We've heard story after story of employees who were invited to a meeting in which they expected a promotion or raise, only to be laid off.

To be clear, although feedback is critical to career and life development, you may not choose to adjust to please everyone; in fact in doing so, you would be managing your brand rather than aligning with your passions. Instead, achieving and sustaining success requires that you know what impact you are having on others, not necessarily to change what you are doing but to know how to progress in alignment with your passions.

* * *

TRUTH #12
Feedback won't just happen; you've got to ask for it.

MYTH #13
Your capacity for achievement is limited.

A number of widely accepted assumptions can unnecessarily limit your ability to achieve. A common assumption is that your capacity to succeed is strictly determined by the genes you inherited and the environment in which you were raised. But such a belief that your potential level of success is limited is a self-fulfilling prophecy—your acceptance of that belief can make it true.

Actually, there are fewer limitations to success than most people realize, and most limitations are self-imposed. It also seems that when we step out to really dream and then share our wildest aspirations with someone else, we are crushed when they respond with disinterest or tell us to "stop dreaming."

Dreaming is good. A key characteristic of many who have achieved career wealth is that they surmounted their current limiting factors, didn't listen to people who thought they were crazy, and achieved things nobody thought they could. The past does not have to dictate the present or future. At any given moment you can decide to separate from those things that limit you and shape your future. Incredible power comes from clear passion and purpose. Most people never experience this or rise above their limiting circumstances. Don't let that stop you.

*   *   *

TRUTH #13
You should focus on your dreams, not on your perceived limitations.

However, dreaming is not enough . . .

MYTH #14
Conceiving it is tantamount to achieving it.

This myth has been popping up in popular literature for decades. Indeed, we have ascribed the title of "visionary" to almost every person who has achieved great stature and wealth in both ancient and modern societies. There is power in a compelling vision and set of aspirations. Indeed, a person or nation without them will perish. However, when applied to personal career success, the overly simple premise that you can achieve what you conceive can cause significant frustration and even be a waste of time.

We have found that many people spend their days, months, and years dreaming of the perfect career and all the wealth, freedom, and/or fame that may go with it, as if dreaming of the perfect life and career will bring them about. For many of these people, it becomes a mental escape, and when they return to focus on their less-than-perfect current reality, it causes frustration. They then feel stuck, unable to emerge from their career quicksand, often blaming circumstances outside their control for their career dissatisfaction.

These people need to learn that a successful career starts with both dreaming and doing, trying and testing, and that vision is often dynamic, changing, and evolving as a person experiments and learns. Indeed, people who achieve career success don't solely dream of what they can achieve; instead, they do what they love and learn along the way. In other words, they are primarily driven to "do" what they love. This replaces lust for a desired future state with love of your current state. This focus on doing is always rewarded with career contentment and often monetary rewards.

*   *   *

TRUTH #14
It is not enough to merely dream of what you love; you must do it.

MYTH #15
It is selfish to do what you want and focus on your career aspirations.

Selfishness has been given a bad rap. Being selfish is not always bad; our free market is built on the concept of enlightened self-interest. There is real power in focusing on what you want. When self-interest is pursued within the parameters of honesty and integrity, it is the source of all significant personal advancement. An athlete cannot perform and win without spending the time and energy to develop his or her muscles and prowess. Similarly, you can't achieve career wealth and maximize your impact on the organization without focusing on yourself.

Related to this is the common belief that you must at times give up your wants and desires for the team. Whether it is an extended assignment nobody else wants or assuming a dead-end role because your manager saw you as the easiest person to tap on the shoulder, it will be better for the company and you if you say no. We have seen this time and again—you will be a much better contributor, and thus team player, when you focus on doing those things you personally love and are passionate about. Solely focusing on what others want from you to be seen as a "team player" will reduce your energy and contribution, making you even less of a team player. So, if you want to maximize your impact on the organization and others, use the organization to realize your personal career passions.

* * *

TRUTH #15
It's good for you to revel in your selfishness, and it's good for the organization.

MYTH #16
You must "pay your dues" before you can advance.

This myth assumes that there is a politically correct time and place for advancement. This is predicated on an invisible set of criteria dictated outside your sphere of control. This is a little bit like waiting on the runway for the perfect conditions for takeoff. You may have to wait a long time, and the perfect weather conditions may never emerge. If you are a good pilot and have an airworthy plane, you should be able to take off in all kinds of weather and reach your desired destination on time and with ease.

Unfortunately, many people find themselves completing meaningless work as a rite of passage. For others, much of their career has been dominated by completing meaningless work, continually paying their dues hoping that one day they will be worthy enough to do the more meaningful work. The "paying dues" construct has led most people to waste much of their career life. Meaningless work does nothing to advance your career wealth, and once you have found your passions and assertively fill your life with work you find meaningful, the meaningless work will fall to someone who can find meaning in it.

* * *

TRUTH #16
Paying your dues truly is a waste of time.

These myths and truths can be liberating as they serve to free you from the false beliefs that bottle you up and ensure that your career success is left to others. It's important that you take them seriously. If you skimmed through these myths and truths quickly, go back and read them again. As you do so, take the time to contemplate each one. Which ones support or contradict the beliefs you listed in Discovery Exercise 2?

Almost guaranteed, this list of career myths and truths exposed some false assumptions you had about career success. This is good, as it may help explain any career angst you may have been experiencing. Demolishing false beliefs is at the source of true career wealth, so let it happen. If you internalized these truths and read no more of this book, your career success would be significantly improved and you would be managing your career in a much more enlightened and effective way. Again, these are foundational truths—things that are true in every age regardless of the fads and clichés of the day. This is an important first phase in building a career of purpose and passion.

Unfortunately, given the popularity of many of these myths, millions of people are building their career on a delimiting premise, thus bound never to realize the sustained fulfillment and wealth that come from building a career on assumptions aligned with the principles of career wealth. That is why adopting these foundational truths will put you on a less traveled yet more enlightened career path.

However, your successful career journey requires more than these sixteen truths. It also requires an organizing set of principles that can take you through a sequential process for finding and achieving your own version of career wealth in your organization.

The Career Wealth Model

This road to career wealth is represented by what we call the Career Wealth Model (see figure 1). It is a road we have traveled ourselves, along with others who have realized career wealth. Nevertheless, it is still a road less traveled.

As shown, achieving career wealth begins at the core of the model, the "Career Foundation"—or, more specifically, with your heart. Here you must identify those things you are most passionate about and what each does for you personally. We call the underlying needs that drive your passions your "passionate core." Your passionate core comprises the two to five needs that must find expression in your life and career and, indeed, will create the energy and passion to create your career success.

Figure 1: Career Wealth Model

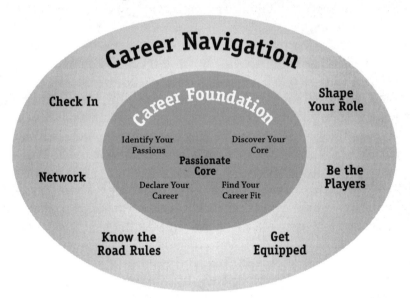

Once your passionate core needs are identified, you will use them as criteria to evaluate and select your career work, that is, to find your career fit. Identifying your passionate core and career fit is work done by yourself and for yourself as you form your career foundation.

Just as a house requires a strong foundation to stand, your career wealth must be built on this strong personal foundation. If you bypass this internal work, career success will not come from solid ground and will not emanate from the power of your heart and passions. In part 1 of this book, "Your Career Foundation," you will uncover and align your career choices with what you love and need in your organization by completing the following four steps:

- **Step 1:** Identify Your Passions

- **Step 2:** Discover Your Core

- **Step 3:** Find Your Career Fit

- **Step 4:** Declare Your Career

The outer band of the Career Wealth Model is called "Career Navigation." The six practices of career wealth listed in this band will help you gain recognition and reward in your organization. In part 2, "Your Career Navigation," you will learn how to put each of these practices into action. You might be tempted to simply bypass the four foundational steps in part 1 and go straight to part 2, as adopting these practices would lead almost immediately to greater acceptance in your work and organization. However, your career wealth must first be built on the stability and energy supplied by your passionate core. If you bypass this internal work, your career success will not come from the source of your power—your passions. Instead of deriving energy from your passions, you will be playing to an audience, always seeking validation from the organization and people you work with. You will rarely be fulfilled and you will never achieve and contribute all you can. Our advice is to concentrate on the internal work first, as sustained career wealth works from the inside out.

To aid in your understanding and application of the inner core and the outer band of the model, we offer a running example and a personal application exercise after each principle and practice. This will allow you to go from understanding to doing to living the principles and practices of career wealth. We hope you stop to take the time to apply these principles to yourself. It will change your career and your life.

SUMMARY

- Like most people, you probably have some degree of frustration with your career.

- There are few formal courses on career success; it's not taught in the high school or college curriculum, and the advice you receive from managers and mentors is often toxic.

- Career assumptions drive behaviors, which drive career results. Career wealth results from correct assumptions on how to achieve it.

- Adopting the sixteen career truths sets the foundation for your career wealth, releasing you from much of the conventional wisdom that can lead to wasted effort and frustration.

CAREER MYTHS	CAREER TRUTHS
MYTH #1 You must manage your image—be your own brand.	**TRUTH #1** You must be yourself and do what you love!
MYTH #2 The company will take care of you.	**TRUTH #2** You are your own company—take care of yourself.
MYTH #3 To get ahead, you just need to do a good job.	**TRUTH #3** Politics are inevitable—you must learn how to navigate them.
MYTH #4 It is important to have work/life balance.	**TRUTH #4** It's not about work/life balance; it's about finding your life's work.
MYTH #5 Company decisions are made rationally.	**TRUTH #5** Both rational and nonrational thinking are always present and necessary.

MYTH #6 You will get ahead by doing what key managers in your organization want (the "yes-person" syndrome).

TRUTH #6 Being a yes-person will limit and frustrate you in your career.

MYTH #7 Career paths are predictable.

TRUTH #7 There may not be a traditional career path that aligns with your passions—don't let that stop you.

MYTH #8 Career progression requires a formal career path.

TRUTH #8 You can't fully plan a great career—so be ready to improvise.

MYTH #9 Once stuck or stereotyped within an organization, there is nothing you can do about it.

TRUTH #9 You must focus on the work, not others' perceptions of you.

MYTH #10 You need to find a career doing what you are good at.

TRUTH #10 You must find a career doing what you love.

MYTH #11 Rocking the boat will sink your career.

TRUTH #11 If the boat is rocking, you might as well try to enjoy the ride.

MYTH #12 Someone will tell you if you are performing poorly or do not have a future with the company.

TRUTH #12 Feedback won't just happen; you've got to ask for it.

MYTH #13 Your capacity for achievement is limited.

TRUTH #13 You should focus on your dreams, not on your perceived limitations.

CAREER MYTHS	CAREER TRUTHS
MYTH #14 Conceiving it is tantamount to achieving it.	**TRUTH #14** It is not enough to merely dream of what you love; you must do it.
MYTH #15 It is selfish to do what you want and focus on your career aspirations.	**TRUTH #15** It's good for you to revel in your selfishness, and it's good for the organization.
MYTH #16 You must "pay your dues" before you can advance.	**TRUTH #16** Paying your dues truly is a waste of time.

The Career Wealth Model provides a path to sustained career success. The rest of the book is dedicated to helping you follow it.

Part 1

Your Career

Foundation

Four Steps for Starting on the Inside

I respect the man who knows distinctly what he wishes. . . .
Mischief . . . arises from . . . men not sufficiently understand[ing]
their own aims. They . . . build a tower, and spend no more labor
on the foundation than would be necessary to erect a hut.
—*Johann Wolfgang von Goethe*

All structures, whether they are physical or intellectual, have to rest on something. They need a guiding force and foundation. Whether it be the housing structure you live in, or your own personal operative thinking pattern, the foundation sets the pattern of behaviors and ultimately the level and pattern of results. As in trying to transform the fundamental shape of a building, you can't transform your career without exploring and reconstructing the foundation upon which it is built.

Establishing a career foundation begins by defining career success, what we have termed *career wealth*. Throughout this book, when we refer to *career* we do not mean a formal set of roles and titles that an organization may bestow. Instead, *career* is used to describe your life's work, plus the ability to bring the things you love into your daily work and find deep fulfillment. As stated, this book rests on the principle that the degree to which your work is aligned with your loves will directly determine your career wealth and fulfillment. Achieving career wealth does not mean your work will always be fun or easy; in fact at times it may be very challenging. When you have achieved career wealth, you are working on all cylinders as your organization supports you, and you are passionate about what you do. Your energy and success feed off each other, generating better-than-expected rewards and ever-increasing opportunities. When this happens you begin each day excited to begin work, and the work itself brings out the best in you.

You will find truly successful people in your organization who have achieved this form of career wealth, where personal passions are fully supported and rewarded. They realize that they don't have to give up what they love to be accepted and successful. Instead, they have clarity about what they love, which has been at the center of their career success. Career passion, fulfillment, and success go hand-in-hand.

The examples of people who have achieved and sustained career wealth are endless and represent all types of organizations and career pursuits. Whether it's Bill Gates, Colin Powell, Carly Fiorina, or the less public yet successful people you know, they all got there by achieving two things: a deep awareness of the things they love to do and key skills for navigating effectively within an organization. In other words, they find what they love and effectively work within their organization so that they are rewarded for constantly doing what they love.

In part 1, you'll find that the journey to real career wealth starts with a deep connection with your passions, those things you find most fulfilling and most want to achieve. Aligning these passions with your work leads to a career of personal meaning, fulfillment, and great rewards.

Achieving real career wealth requires you to explore your passions, identifying those things you love and most care about. This comes from scratching below the surface and discovering the source of your passions, what we call the *passionate core*. When you

Figure 2: Your Career Foundation

discover your core, it can have a profound impact on your life and career, as you better understand what you need and love, and bring that deliberately into your work.

Most people never pursue this deep inner territory. Instead they settle on the external symbols of success such as the job title, compensation, and perks. These organization rewards should instead be a manifestation of the pursuit of your own passions, not the driving reason you go to work every day. Titles and rewards, when not grounded in your passions, are hollow and will leave you unsatisfied. It is like looking at the picture of the steak rather than tasting it—it may appear delicious but you are still left hungry.

As described earlier, discovering your passionate core and finding your career fit are the two important components of your career foundation, which together will enable you to find what you love (see figure 2). To help you establish your personal career foundation, we will guide you through a four-step process for finding and defining the career you will create for yourself. Completing these four steps will set the foundation upon which you ultimately will achieve career wealth.

- **Step 1:** Identify Your Passions

- **Step 2:** Discover Your Core

- **Step 3:** Find Your Career Fit

- **Step 4:** Declare Your Career

Establishing your career foundation is personal work. You will accomplish it primarily on your own. After you have completed this first part of the journey, you will move on to six practices described in part 2 to help you take action. Adopting any one of these practices will increase your influence and capability. However, if they are not based on a firm career foundation made up of these four steps, you will not realize sustained career wealth. So resist the temptation to go straight to the second part of the book. Once you are clear about what you love to do, your career expectations increase exponentially. Learning and using the six practices will enable you to fulfill your passions within an organization. But again, do the internal work in this part first.

Step 1

Identify Your
Passions

---

*In order to create there must be a dynamic force,
and what force is more potent than love?*
—Igor Stravinsky

At the heart of your energy, power, and life are the things you love—the source of your passions. Uncovering and aligning with what you love brings passion into your life and career, resulting in career wealth. This simple truth, coupled with the concept that you can do it in your present organization, is the core premise of this book. In this chapter you will take the first step in establishing your career foundation by identifying your passions.

Career Wealth from
Unleashed Passion

Identifying your passions and aligning with them is a requirement for true sustained success in a career or any endeavor in life, and it is profound and deeply personal. Everyone has unique passions.

But rather than explore what is really important to us, we often adopt and conform to the desires and expectations of our managers, teachers, parents, and those we admire and are closest to. In doing so, we trade passions for conformance, acceptance, and predictability. This is done without our even knowing it. As a result, we never find the true meaning, fulfillment, and success we so want in our work and life.

Expressing Passion in Different Ways

People often confuse passion with open and frenetic expression. We have all seen and known the "creative types" who are constantly open with their feelings and passions and bring this into the work they do. But passion can also be manifested through quiet and intensive resolve. The truth is, passion is the force behind bringing into being what we love. It is attached to the core of who we are and what we want to achieve in our lives. It is intense. And how it translates into life and work will vary from person to person.

Our loves bring out the best in us. When we love something, it conjures up real passion and emotion and we want to share it with others. Whether we are passionate about opera, reading, cabinetmaking, computer programming, or sailing, it is something we look forward to and gladly do for no financial reward.

Don't confuse love with lust. When we lust for something, we constantly reach for that elusive "thing" while never fully realizing a sense of fulfillment or success. Whether it is an organization title, acclaim, or money, once achieved it rarely delivers happiness. Once on the lust-driven career track, it's often hard to get off because of the false belief that the goal is just over the hill.

In most organizations, the formal career planning and compensation systems are based on the assumption that bigger titles, fatter paychecks, and more strokes from the boss are all that is needed to motivate people. There is nothing inherently wrong with titles, money, and recognition; however, if that is the only way for people to be motivated, it underestimates what's required to unleash the power of people's spirit and passions.

People in organizations commonly don't question this, instead focusing on the rewards and recognition the organization has to offer, without asking themselves and the organization to align with their passions. Unfortunately, the lust-driven career path has become the norm.

A few cutting-edge companies understand that people need more than titles, money, and recognition. They understand that people need to bring what they love to work. These companies have processes for helping people explore and build their passions and for helping employees fueled by their unique passions to bring greater value to the company. Many of these companies find themselves on the lists of top companies to work for. Tapping into people's natural energy translates into solid competitive advantage.

You are probably not in an organization that actively asks you what you are passionate about, but you can still bring your passions to your work and be rewarded for it.

Making a Choice

The bottom line is that we need to learn and understand our unique passions. While we become adept at responding to the needs and expectations of people important to us, we rarely take the time to fully understand and get in touch with what we love. This lack of self-awareness is the reason most people never really attain a sense of career wealth. But those who have achieved sustained success in any endeavor have lived by this principle—they know their passions and have made a deep choice to realize them. One of these is Michael Dell.

MICHAEL DELL _____

Michael Dell, founder, chairman, and CEO of Dell Computer Corporation, related his struggle and determination to realize his passion for starting a computer company. As an eighteen-year-old freshman at the University of Texas, Dell began his computer business without informing his disapproving parents. As his grades slipped, his parents found out about his business ventures and confronted him about his "misplaced priorities." As they pleaded with him to concentrate on his studies, they asked

the age-old question—"What do you want to do with your life?"
Dell answered, "I want to compete with IBM!"

Source: Michael Dell, *Direct from Dell: Strategies That Revolutionized an Industry* (New York: Harper-Collins, 1999), 10.

At eighteen years old Dell had made a deep choice to make his passion his life work. The rest is history. Dell Computer Corporation has grown to be a multibillion-dollar company, revolutionizing the way goods are sold and distributed. Dell himself has achieved extreme financial wealth, but more important, he has achieved real career wealth as he has created a career aligned with his passionate core—computers, efficiency, and cutting-edge growth.

Once you make a deep choice, it will reorient your career—focusing your attention and capabilities on the realization of your passions. Opportunities will appear that you would never have dreamed of; you will begin to believe the saying, "When the student is ready, the master appears."

Bringing Your Passions to Work

When it comes to your career, passion is at the heart—everything comes from it. It will get you out of bed, get you to work, and determine how much you enjoy and are successful in your chosen profession.

Companies are not built to align with your passions. Within any company, we typically organize our time to meet the needs of those who have the ability to reward and punish us, regardless of our personal passions. However, those who have true career wealth know that there is incredible power in knowing their passions and aligning daily actions and experiences within the company with them.

If we are not clear about our passions, the company will dictate what we should care about and do. When we find ourselves spending time working on things we are not passionate about, the focus moves to the fulfillment of lower-level needs: money, food, safety.

When this happens, we are not tapping into the heart—the source of distinctive and creative energy.

True career wealth often means you are no longer a "company person," but rather you become a unique and influential person within the company. Aligning with your passions at work puts you in the driver's seat. It represents a fundamental shift—from reacting and responding to the expectations of key people in your company to bringing your whole person and creating and shaping your future. When aligned with your passions, you will set in motion a direction and orientation that will enable you to achieve that which most matters to you. Sometimes aligning with your passions requires you to make nonrational career choices. This was the case with an associate we will call Len.

LEN

As a midlevel manager at Keith Construction, a residential construction company in Alberta, Canada, Len had to choose between two promotions. His choices were to lead either the company's design group or its sales group. Len's passion was design, but he felt the sales role offered more exposure and thus a more direct path to a senior leadership role. For him the options were to follow his personal passion or to chase the organization symbols of success.

Len eventually followed his passions and took the design role. Not only did he enjoy his new role, but it did not end up being the career dead end he had envisioned. As the housing market changed, so did the company's priorities. The design group took center stage and so did Len's career as he eventually moved into an executive leadership role and completed his career as the company's president.

Career paths are in a constant state of flux; opportunities open and close. Making career choices without tapping into your true passions often leads to unfulfilled expectations and frustration. When aligning with your passions you may experience some short-term pain and adjustment. In the mid to long term, though, you never lose, as you will be doing what you love and, ultimately, you will be in an organization that will rally around it and reward it.

Building the Foundation

Building the foundation is up to you. There are two simple but profound decisions necessary to align with your passions: the decision to *own your life* and the decision to *identify and declare your life passions*.

Deciding to Own Your Life

You must choose to live your life, not someone else's, or what you think others expect of you. This means knowing what you want and living with the consequences of the choices you make. Your choices may inadvertently disappoint people in your life and lead to significant changes in what you are doing. However, once you make the choice, the sense of liberation you will experience will make any short-term resistance well worth it.

This doesn't have to be a choice you make out of dissatisfaction with your current state. However, if you don't take ownership of your life, you will have periods of quiet desperation and a sense of low fulfillment because you have abdicated your life to others. The decision is up to you. Although taking ownership of your life is not a cure-all, your increased sense of fulfillment will help surmount the normal frustrations in any career choice. Don't let career wealth elude you. Start by taking full ownership of your life.

Everyone who has achieved sustained career wealth has made the critical decision to own their life. Many times they can identify the time and place they decided to make their own choices and take control of their destiny. Carly Fiorina is one good example.

CARLY FIORINA _____

Carly Fiorina, former chairman and CEO of Hewlett-Packard Corporation, relates the moment she took control of her destiny. After graduating from college, she responded to the urgings of her father, who was a judge, and entered law school at

UCLA. On the surface this would appear to be a great career decision for an ambitious young person. However, she now states that she was miserable and that she was only attending law school to fulfill her father's wishes. Then on a visit home during her first semester, Fiorina states, "I can tell you exactly which shower tile I was staring at in my parents' bathroom when it hit me like a bolt of lightning: It's my life. I can do what I want. It was an epiphany for me . . . I got out of the shower. And I walked downstairs and said, 'I quit.'"

The rest is history. In the months after taking ownership of her life, Fiorina discovered and aligned her passions with her career. Two decades after that defining moment she was heading up a 72 billion dollar company as the most senior female corporate executive in history.

Source: Peter Burrows, *Backfire* (Hoboken, NJ: John Wiley & Sons, 2003), 38.

People who have achieved sustained career wealth across every occupation echo Fiorina's experience. From billionaire entrepreneur and Dallas Mavericks owner Mark Cuban to George Bush Jr. and Bill Clinton, they all point to a time when they chose to be the primary creator of their life and stop living the life that someone else, or society, expected.

To be sure, while making the choice to own your life is necessary, initially it may feel risky. Many will not make this choice because they feel that they must settle for what life gives them, that they can't really have what they love. For others it is fear of failure that prevents them from stepping out and making this critical choice. There is no guarantee in life, but if it is what your heart is telling you, then listen! Your heart provides the best answers to the biggest decisions in your life. So cast off fear and set sail . . . your heart matters!

Identifying Your Passions

Once you have made the choice to be the primary owner of your life, move your focus to the things that energize you. Identify and align with your passions.

Think about it: Everyone you know who has achieved true career wealth has declared their passions. They have not settled for a "job," but rather emphatically brought their passions into their work and made it an extension of their life mission. From architect Frank Lloyd Wright to the legendary radio host Paul Harvey or any number of successful professionals, they all want to keep on working and creating even when they have more money than they will ever need. The reason is simple: Their job is not "work"; it's what they love.

Begin to discover what you really love by answering the questions in Discovery Exercise 3.

DISCOVERY EXERCISE 3

Discovering What You Love to Do

Directions: Take a few minutes to consider each question below and record your answers in the space allowed.

1. If you knew you had five years left before you died, how would you spend your time?

   What would you want to do and achieve?

2. If you were independently wealthy, how would you spend your time?

   What would you want to do and achieve?

In the first scenario, your time is precious. After all, you have only five years left to live. In the second scenario, you have complete discretion over how you spend your time; that is, you don't have to work for money. Noticing the recurring types of things you would do in these scenarios will help you to discover what you love. These are the critical things you have a personal passion for. Now consider:

- How do the activities you've listed compare to how you currently spend your time?
- Are you able to bring these loves and passions into your daily work, or does your job "get in the way"?

To repeat, passions are the things you love. They are part of your essence and life force, not to be confused with things you desire. Instead, these are the things closest to your heart that inspire and excite you. The sample list below of deeply personal yet easily identifiable passions will help you to complete Discovery Exercise 4, which follows.

EXAMPLE

Passions: What I Really Love to Do

- Enjoying the outdoors: wildlife, mountains, open spaces
- Spending time with my family
- Working on house projects: building and improving home and property
- Solving business problems: developing solutions
- Teaching: both working with students in a classroom and tutoring someone one-on-one
- Learning: reading and discussing new ideas and concepts
- Keeping fit: running and working out alone on my own time
- Enjoying music: appreciating and singing along; going to live performances
- Reading the morning newspaper: using downtime to keep up with current events

DISCOVERY EXERCISE 4

Passions: What I Really Love to Do

Directions: In the space below, write the words and phrases that immediately come to mind when you ask yourself, "What do I really love to do?" Record them quickly without qualifying them. They may come from any part of your life—home, work, relationships, activities, and so on. Don't spend too much time on it. If you have to think hard after the first five to ten things, you've gotten beyond your true loves.

Going Deeper to Your Passion Source

If it were as simple as identifying the things you are passionate about and then finding a way to make a living by doing them, we could stop here and let you be on your way. However, passions are transient. The activities that bring us happiness and even fulfillment can change over time. The things that don't change are the needs these passions fulfill. These needs are the source code we call the passionate core. Identifying your passionate core will provide you with the energy, direction, and flexibility to bring your passions to your work and the organization(s) you choose to be in.

SUMMARY

- At the heart of your energy, power, and life are the things you love—the source of your passions.

- Passion is intense, and how it translates into life and work will vary from person to person.

- Don't confuse love with lust. When we lust for something, we constantly reach for that elusive "thing" but never fully realize a sense of fulfillment or success.

- Those who have achieved sustained success in any endeavor have lived this principle—they know their passions and have made a deep personal choice to realize them.

- If we are not clear about our passions, the company will dictate what we should care about and do.

- Aligning with your passions at work puts you in the driver's seat. It represents a fundamental shift—from reacting and responding to the expectations of key people in your company to bringing your whole person and creating and shaping your future.

- Making career choices without tapping into your true passions often leads to unfulfilled expectations and frustration.

- There are two profound decisions needed to align with your passions: the decision to own your life, and the decision to identify and declare your life passions.

Step 2

Discover

Your Core

Not only can a person filled with passion change the world;
in fact that's the only thing that has.
—Anonymous

Specific passions can come and go at any time in your life. Like you, we have had periods in which we were passionate about activities such as golf, poetry, traveling, and playing the guitar. At the time these were real passions, dominating our thoughts and discretionary time. But these passions are not to be confused with your passionate core. Had we made career choices based on these short-term passions, we would have built our careers on weak foundations. In this chapter you will take the second step in establishing your career foundation by discovering your passionate core.

The relationship of your personal career foundation and your passionate core at the center of the Career Wealth Model are shown in figure 3. The passionate core is made up of the two to five needs that must find expression in your life and career for you to realize sustained energy, passion, and success. These are the

Figure 3: Passionate Core Dynamics

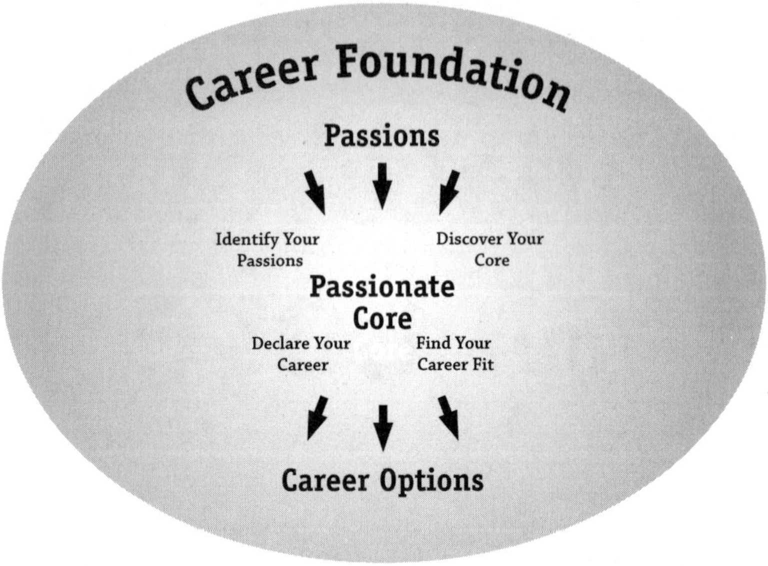

needs that are being fulfilled by the activities you are passionate about. The passionate core needs don't change over time, whereas the activities you are passionate about that fulfill these needs likely will.

For example, a friend we'll call Steve was passionate about carpentry, writing, and painting. Each of these activities fulfilled a common need to *create something that lasts*. Understanding this passionate core need provided much more flexibility when exploring career options. If Steve had simply looked at how his passionate core was expressed at that period in his life, he might have felt a need to build homes, write mystery novels, or paint murals to find passion in his work. However, understanding the underlying need allowed him to choose from a wider variety of career and work options that would allow him to create something that lasts. Steve was also able to avoid work opportunities that seemed appealing from the outside—offering money and prestige, for instance—but would frustrate his need to create something that lasts.

How to Discover Your Passionate Core

Discover your passionate core by identifying the things you are passionate about and then for each one asking, "What does this passion do for me personally?" As you complete Discovery Exercises 5 and 6 later in this chapter, you will find that your passions, however few or many, will all lead back to a few critical core needs. These specific needs can be effectively fulfilled in your career and within your organization in a number of ways.

More Career Options from Your Passionate Core

Getting beyond your passionate activities to your passionate core needs is absolutely critical. People we have worked with often point to passions outside the realm of their career choice. Whether it be the accountant who loves travel, the manager who has a passion for gardening, or the schoolteacher who spends all his spare time working on cars, there often appears to be no way for the person to make a living doing what he or she really loves.

Looking deeper at their passionate core reveals that the accountant's love of travel fulfills a core need for freedom and learning; the manager with a passion for gardening has a need to create and grow things; and the schoolteacher who is constantly fixing old cars has a need to make things more efficient and perform better. In each case, discovering their passionate core will provide powerful self-awareness and greater flexibility when finding passion and wealth within an organization. For the accountant it will likely be easier to find a role that offers freedom and learning in her current organization than in a role solely focused on travel and sightseeing. Similarly, the manager and teacher will have a much easier time finding roles in an organization that align with their passionate core.

The multitude of career choices made available by uncovering one's passionate core is illustrated by a colleague of ours we will call Barry.

BARRY

For years Barry had a passion for photography, and he held the false belief that the only thing that would bring him ultimate career fulfillment would be to quit his job and open his own photography studio. Given his highly paid position and the financial needs of his family, he felt making such a move would be too risky and resigned himself to being satisfied with the fulfillment of basic needs—such as a predictable schedule and regular paycheck—that his position provided. This all changed when he identified his passionate core and realized that his love of photography was based on his core need to express himself creatively—something that had been missing from his role for years. He was able to fulfill this need in his current role by getting involved in more ground-floor innovation projects and delegating some of the maintenance activities to others on his staff. The result has been a more fulfilling career.

Uncovering your passionate core can also help you look at your current work in different ways. For many, it reframes their current job, enabling them to bring their heart into the work they have been doing for years. Such was the case with someone we will call Annette.

ANNETTE

Annette was fifty-five years old and, as a tax accountant, had been preparing personal income taxes for two decades. One day, as Annette was preparing income tax forms for coauthor Bill Gargiulo, she shared her dissatisfaction with her heavy workload and the drudgery and monotony of completing endless income tax returns and simply "shuffling paper." In uncovering her passionate core needs, it became clear that she needed to build something tangible, connect with people and their life stories, and complete tasks. For years Annette had been expressing these needs by weaving small baskets, usually with her family and other friends.

One day when Bill and Annette were discussing her core needs, she had a breakthrough. She realized that each of her passionate core needs could find expression in her current role. She was indeed taking raw ingredients such as receipts and pay stubs and creating a tax return, and each completed tax return gave her the needed sense of completion. In the process she could learn about each person, their desires, and their story since she last saw them the year before. In thinking about her work in this way she realized that completing a tax return was like completing a basket. This realization changed Annette immediately. It made her role much more meaningful to her and allowed her to bring her passionate core into her current work by focusing on helping people and creating excellent tax returns instead of simply shuffling paper. Annette went from completing her work out of a sense of duty and obligation to choosing her work as a natural extension of what she needs and loves. This is called the passionate core "reframe."

Sometimes aligning with one's passionate core motivates a significant change in role, industry, or location. Such was the case with another person we worked with we will call James.

JAMES

Based on a felt passion for adventure, James joined the U.S. Army with the hope of seeing new places and "being all he could be." However, he became disillusioned with the perceived rules and constraints of military life. Once in touch with his passionate core, he realized he really needed independence and a sense of control over his destiny. Based on this, he finished his military commitment and started an Internet services business. Although starting his business has been challenging, he is realizing fulfillment and at the time of the writing of this book his company is experiencing excellent growth.

James did not have to move out of a formal military career to find fulfillment of his core needs. Even in an environment and culture as controlled as the military, there are roles for people within the whole spectrum of core needs. By using the practices outlined in part 2 of this book, James could have carved a career of health and wealth in the military. However, the most important thing is that James is aligned with his core needs and is loving it.

These and numerous other examples point to the fact that career wealth comes from alignment with one's passionate core. As people become clear and focused on expressing their few critical core needs in their work, it generates real energy. Like fire carried by the winds, as this energy is unleashed it will create more energy. We are all interconnected. When your passions are focused and unleashed, they affect people and circumstances you can't know, surfacing opportunities you could not have imagined.

Fruits of the Passionate Core

We cannot overstate the importance of uncovering and aligning with your passionate core. The degree to which you understand the needs behind your loves and passions and deliberately bring those into your work will directly determine your level of career wealth. And since we are holistic beings, the fulfillment we derive from our work affects every other aspect of our life including our spirit and body.

Now review Discovery Exercise 1, "Career Wealth Indicator," on pages 4–6. The descriptions in the right-hand column are a partial list of the fruits of the passionate core. You are aligned with your passionate core when these descriptors accurately describe how you feel about your work and career at any given time. They describe the ongoing state for the person who has achieved career wealth.

With your passionate core as your source, you are able to shape sustained career wealth. Other standard career solutions such as greater work/life balance, a defined career path, and better pay may reenergize you in the short term; however, the effect will wear off quickly as your level of real career wealth is determined by your level of alignment with your passionate core.

BILL GARGIULO

On a personal level, as an author and business professional, Bill made a deep decision in 1992. Upon uncovering his passionate core needs for freedom, service, and the space to think and create, he actively worked to bring these into his work and deliberately backed away from his previous desires for the organizational symbols of success, such as a more prestigious title. He discovered and deployed the practices covered in part 2, "Your Career Navigation," and found previously unknown success. He found that people trusted him more and reacted positively to his renewed energy. He was more effective as an employee and more fulfilled as a person while being rewarded by the organization in ways he probably never would have had he continued to focus on simply getting ahead. Bill saw that other aspects of his life were also positively affected, including his health, as he has gone over a decade without being sick. He finds great meaning in the work he does, and his level of personal assurance and confidence is consistently higher than before he made this choice. There is real power in alignment with one's passionate core.

People whose career and life have changed through alignment with their passionate core say they experience freedom and personal insight, with an appetite for endless possibilities. Minor irritations such as backaches and headaches either go away or become insignificant. After their alignment, they need less sleep, and the sleep they do get is much more restful. In each case their spirit has been validated, filled, and allowed to soar.

Your spirit and body are connected. Doing what you love feeds your spirit and strengthens your body. For those who experience a significant shift in alignment the change can be remarkable—their stature and countenance tell those around them they are filled with hope and engagement. People notice immediately. Nothing is more compelling and energizing than seeing someone do what they love.

Getting to Your Core

Uncovering your passionate core begins by looking at each of your passions and asking yourself, "What does this do for me personally?" The example below lists the needs at the source of the sample passions listed earlier. Reviewing them will help you to complete Discovery Exercise 5, which follows.

EXAMPLE
My Needs

Passion:
Enjoying the outdoors: wildlife, mountains, open spaces

Needs:
- A feeling of being alive—opening my mind to greater possibilities
- A sense of freedom
- Reverence for, and inspiration from, natural beauty
- Time alone to think

Passion:
Working on house projects: building and improving home and property

Needs:
- Time alone to think
- Personal expression—putting my personality into my surroundings
- Creating something that lasts
- A feeling of completion when I'm done

Passion:

Solving business problems: developing solutions

Needs:
- Reaffirming my ability to think
- Mental challenges—expanding my ability to think
- Creating/developing something that makes a tangible difference

Passion:

Teaching: both working with students in a classroom and tutoring someone one-on-one

Needs:
- Seeing people learn, develop, and grow
- Learning and new ideas

Passion:

Reading the morning newspaper: using downtime to keep up with current events

Needs:
- Generating new thoughts and ideas
- Absorbing new facts and information
- Time alone to think

DISCOVERY EXERCISE 5
My Needs

Directions: Enter each of the passions you identified in Discovery Exercise 4 (p. 46). Then fill in your needs by answering the question "What does this passion do for me personally?"

Passion:

Needs:

-
-
-
-

Passion:

Needs:

-
-
-
-

Passion:

Needs:

-
-
-
-

Passion:

Needs:

-
-
-
-

Passion:

Needs:

-
-
-
-

Passion:

Needs:

-
-
-
-

Passion:

Needs:

-
-
-
-

Passion:

Needs:

-
-
-
-

For the passions you listed in Discovery Exercise 5, you recorded one or more needs that each fulfills. You are likely to notice two to five needs that are listed more than once. These recurring needs are your *passionate core needs*. These passionate core needs are the source of most if not all your passions. Consider each of them and take the time to discuss them with someone who knows you well to further clarify and define what each need does for you, or why it is so important to you. Below is a sample list of the core needs from the previous example. Discovery Exercise 6 follows.

EXAMPLE
List of Passionate Core Needs

- Freedom to think, learn, and follow my instincts
- Teaching and developing others—I love to see people and things progress and grow
- Mental challenges—I always want to be learning new things
- Creating and developing new things that will last—from conception to implementation—as opposed to maintaining things

---

By the end of this exercise you will have defined your passionate core. These are the elements that you will want to organize your work around to ensure that you achieve sustained career wealth.

DISCOVERY EXERCISE 6
My Passionate Core Needs

Directions: Review your list of core needs in Discovery Exercise 5 (pp. 58–59). You are likely to find a few consistent passionate themes. These are your critical core needs. Record these below with a one- or two-sentence description of each.

Passionate Core Need:

Passionate Core Need:

Passionate Core Need:

Passionate Core Need:

Congratulations! By completing Discovery Exercise 6, you have worked to achieve a rare and powerful level of self-awareness. You have uncovered the needs that must be met for you to feel whole and be your best. You are now ready to go on to step 3, "Find Your Career Fit."

SUMMARY

- Your passionate core needs are the needs that are being fulfilled by the activities you are passionate about and that must find expression in your life and career for you to realize sustained energy, passion, and success.

- The activities you are passionate about may change over time, but the passionate core needs that drive these needs stay constant.

- Understanding your passionate core needs provides you with greater flexibility in finding a role in your organization in which you will be successful and fulfilled.

- You can identify the needs that drive your passion by asking yourself, "What does this do for me personally?"

- The needs that drive many if not all your passions are your passionate core needs.

Step 3

Find Your Career Fit

The wisest men follow their own direction.
—Euripides

In a very real way, your career work is your life work. Determining the venue where you spend most of your productive life, your career choices and decisions have a profound impact on who you are and will become as a person. This is why it's imperative that you take ownership of your career by ensuring that your work and life align with your passionate core.

Once identified, your passionate core needs set the direction for evaluating career and life choices. Whether your core needs are stability, learning, and improving things or creativity, expression, and the spotlight, your life and work should revolve around finding positive expression for these things. It's finding activities and venues from which you can get the most, and just as important, to which you can give the most. In this chapter you will take the third step in establishing your career foundation by finding your career fit.

Assessing Current Alignment

This career decision-making process is launched by assessing your current fit. Specifically, you need to use your newly uncovered passionate core needs to assess your level of alignment in your current work; that is, to what degree do your core needs find expression in your work?

Your passionate core holds the key to your passion and energy. Assessing the degree to which your passionate core needs are fulfilled in your current role will help you to better understand why you do or do not find fulfillment and wealth in this role, and what career elements need to be in place going forward to find your career fit.

A direct and positive correlation exists between finding expression for your passionate core needs and the level of career wealth you are experiencing. So, if your core needs are currently finding expression in your work, you are probably experiencing a sense of career wealth; whereas if your core needs are not finding expression in your current role, you are likely hanging on at best and really depressed at worst. Whatever your current level of alignment and career wealth, the Discovery Exercises in this chapter will help you to find your career fit. You never know what may bubble up.

You are now ready to generate and evaluate career options. You should enter this phase open to all possibilities and alternatives, knowing that your ultimate career choices will come only after you've looked at all the ways you can feasibly bring your passionate core into your career. At the end, you may end up staying in your current career or you may make significant career changes. Whatever your ultimate career choice, you will only be committed to it if you have gone through the process with an open mind, honestly looking at and evaluating all alternatives. This begins by assessing your current career fit. Review the example on the following page and then complete Discovery Exercise 7, which follows.

EXAMPLE

Assessing Your Career Fit

Passionate Core Needs	Level of Current Career Fit

Level of Current Career Fit

1 ——————————— 5

Requirement not met — Requirement fully met

Core Need:

Freedom to think, learn, and follow my instincts

1 ② 3 4 5

Why: I'm under huge pressure to improve sales numbers, with little staff to help and almost no time to think or try new things.

Core Need:

Teaching and developing others—I love to see people and things progress and grow

1 ② 3 4 5

Why: I can teach some new salespeople, but it's rare and I don't have much time for it.

Core Need:

Mental challenges—I always want to be learning new things

1 2 ③ 4 5

Why: I have some important problems to help solve, but they are not new, and I am not in a position to address their root causes.

Core Need:

Creating and developing new things that will last—from conception to implementation—as opposed to maintaining things

1 ② 3 4 5

Why: My job is mostly short-term focused, but I have some flexibility to help create new programs and implement new ideas.

Conclusion: The individual's current role is not fulfilling his or her passionate core needs.

Assessing Your Career Fit

Directions: Under the heading "Passionate Core Needs," list the core needs you identified in Discovery Exercise 6 (p. 61). Then, under the heading "Level of Current Career Fit," assess the degree to which each core need is (was) being fulfilled in your current (previous) role, on a scale of 1–5, by circling the number that best matches your assessment.

Passionate Core Needs	**Level of Current Career Fit**
	1 ————————————— 5
	Requirement Requirement
	not met fully met
Core Need:	1 2 3 4 5
	Why:
Core Need:	1 2 3 4 5
	Why:
Core Need:	1 2 3 4 5
	Why:
Core Need:	1 2 3 4 5
	Why:

Based on this analysis, to what degree are (were) your core needs finding expression in your work? How does this explain your level of fulfillment?

Scanning Career Alternatives

Finding a career begins with open thinking, looking at all possible ways to carve a career out of your passionate core. As discussed before, by focusing on the needs you have in your passionate core, you will likely find there are a number of ways to express your core needs both inside and outside your organization. In generating alternatives it's important that you take the time to explore a lot of possibilities. Although you may not ultimately choose some of the more far-out or extreme alternatives, considering and thinking about them will open up your mind and allow for other connections and opportunities to bubble up. In generating alternatives, the key question you must answer is, "Given my passionate core, in what kinds of work would I find the most fulfillment?"

In answering this question be sure not to add the additional qualifying question: "And what kinds of work will make me sufficient money?" This question automatically and needlessly limits your choices and opportunities. And, it neglects this important fact: There is enough room in society and in organizations to make a great living doing what you love. In fact, people in organizations will rally around those people who declare what they love to do, even if what they love is different or nontraditional.

Such was the case with someone we will call Anne.

ANNE

Anne was a human resources professional with a large financial institution. After identifying her passionate core needs as being on the cutting edge of research, solving complex problems, and organizing, she finally understood why she did not like the role she had held for the last three years as a human resources manager. This role involved lots of meetings and quick decisions, with little time to focus on any one issue. Anne was tired of always applying "half-baked" thinking and craved time to really research and solve something. Her two-year-old hobby of solving complex word games was likely fueled by these passionate core needs that were not being met at work. Her challenge was to bring her core needs to work every day.

With the possibilities provided by uncovering her passion-
ate core, Anne scanned the horizon of careers. She considered
everything from quitting her job and obtaining a Ph.D. at a
research-oriented university to writing crossword puzzles to
becoming a Six Sigma expert in her company to becoming an
actuary. In this exercise of trying to paint the perfect role she
talked to some co-workers and family members, one of which
suggested she consider a role in compensation and benefits. As
a compensation and benefits professional, she would not have
to leave the Human Resources department. Anne thought this
was a lower-risk strategy, but she wasn't sure it would truly
fulfill all her passionate core needs.

Anne shared this with her manager and elicited her help
in finding the right role. Together they found a more perfect
position for Anne—helping lead strategic initiatives for the
Human Resources department. This was a new and much-
needed position that drew upon all of Anne's core needs. In this
role she has filled a void and added significant value in the
organization, all while experiencing tremendous career fulfill-
ment. She transformed her career and is doing what she loves.
She got to this point by exploring all her alternatives and elic-
iting others' help. In doing so she also drew upon an important
principle: People will rally around and support those who
declare their passions and ask for support. Anne also took
action.

Reviewing the next example will help you to generate
your own career options to fulfill core needs in Discovery
Exercise 8, which follows.

EXAMPLE

Generating Career Options to Fulfill Core Needs

Passionate Core Needs from Previous Example

Core Need: Freedom to think, learn, and follow my instincts

Core Need: Teaching and developing others—I love to see people and things progress and grow

Core Need: Mental challenges—I always want to be learning new things

Core Need: Creating and developing new things that will last—from conception to implementation—as opposed to maintaining things

---

Career Options for Fulfilling Passionate Core Needs

1. Quit my job and start teaching high school
2. Keep my job and start teaching junior college in the evenings
3. Move into a sales training and/or coaching role at Company XYZ or somewhere else
4. Start a landscaping business—install lawns, fences, and porches
5. Become a golf pro
6. Teach children's golf and/or soccer, full-time or on weekends
7. Move into a sales management support role—develop a sales team
8. Apply for the fast-track management program at Company XYZ
9. Get into a human resources role to help solve issues and develop people
10. Become a quality consultant in my company—a Six Sigma Black Belt
11. Become an external sales consultant—join an established consulting firm or go out on my own
12. Get a Ph.D. and become a university professor

DISCOVERY EXERCISE 8
Generating Career Options to Fulfill Core Needs

Directions: In the space provided, write a minimum of ten career options for fulfilling the passionate core needs you identified in Discovery Exercise 7 (p. 66).

-
-
-
-
-
-
-
-
-
-

From Thinking to Doing

One reason so many people are dissatisfied with their career is that they spend their life thinking about what could be, merely playing with career options in their mind. Many avoid making a choice because that would take other career options off the table and require them to take real action. However, to achieve career wealth, you will have to make a choice. In doing so it's critical that you be fully committed and proceed with confidence down your chosen trail. In fact, one common element among those who have achieved career wealth is that they have openly declared their career goals and intentions. Their career is their quest, and others are catalyzed as they progress down the career path aligned with their passionate core.

Career Risks and Core Needs Alignment

However, before venturing down your chosen career path it's useful to be conscious of the risks associated with your career decision. When career options appear about equal, take the time to assess the probable change and risks associated with each one. The goal is not to take the easiest, least risky path. Instead, evaluate these elements of your decision, taking them in and finally letting your heart decide.

The Career Risk and Alignment Tool (see p. 73) may be useful for evaluating each career option. With this tool you will look at each option in terms of the amount of risk it will impose and its alignment with your passionate core. Risk denotes anything that is new or unknown. For example, moving to a new company and acquiring new skills are types of risks. To be clear, risks are not bad; they are even necessary as they energize and focus us. However, it is good practice to take risk into consideration when evaluating career options.

The Career Risk and Alignment Tool doesn't give you the final answer on where to take your career, but it does provide a powerful perspective to help bring the two critical decision sources—your head and your heart—together in evaluating each option. Using the sample career options listed on page 69, the example on page 72 shows how some of those options might be categorized as higher or lower risks and in higher or lower alignment with passionate core needs in the matrix. Options from the earlier list were selected based on level of excitement generated, using a process that will be described in Discovery Exercise 9, which follows.

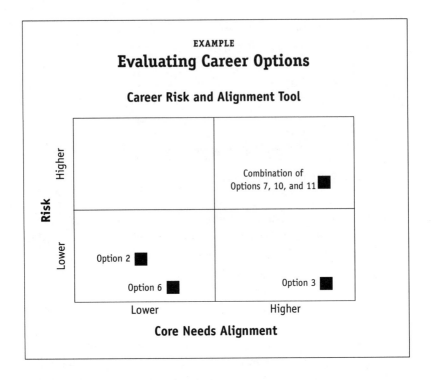

EXAMPLE
Evaluating Career Options

Career Risk and Alignment Tool

Now you are ready to use the Career Risk and Alignment Tool to evaluate the trade-offs of each option.

When choosing your life's work, take the time it requires. Think about these ideas for a few days to see if the initial excitement is sustained. Talk to objective and insightful people, and learn to filter out the noise you will likely hear. Conventional wisdom would have you follow the easier and more predictable path, but the predictable path may not be the one for you. It is your life, your passionate core, and, at the end of the day, your career choice. Follow your heart.

DISCOVERY EXERCISE 9

Evaluating Career Options

Directions: After having generated a variety of career options in Discovery Exercise 8 (p. 70) you can refine the list a little. Look at each option on your list and make a gut check for each one. Cross off the ones that don't excite you and circle the ones that really do. For those that are circled, combine any repetitive opportunities and take one final review to see if there is anything that stands out as being especially aligned with your passionate core. The goal is to identify at least two to eight career options that you want to evaluate further.

Using the matrix below, place each career option in one of the four boxes to show its relative level of alignment with your passionate core and the approximate amount of risk involved.

Career Risk and Alignment Tool

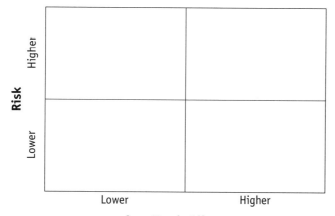

Core Needs Alignment

Once you have positioned your career options in the matrix, consider taking those placed in the top and bottom boxes on the left off your list of potential career options—these options do not provide you with the elements necessary to achieve career wealth. For those options in the top and bottom boxes on the right, consider the degree of risk involved for each. Is an option listed in the top, "Higher Risk" box significantly more aligned with your passionate core needs than any listed in the bottom, "Lower Risk" box?

SUMMARY

- With passionate core needs identified, you are ready to find your career fit. Complete the following three steps:

  1. Assess your current fit—evaluate the level of alignment in your current role with your passionate core needs.

  2. Generate career options—look at the multitude of different ways that you could bring your passionate core needs into your work and your organization.

  3. Evaluate career options—use the Career Risk and Alignment Tool to evaluate the career options that excite you.

- After completing the analysis in these three steps, listen to your heart and make a decision.

Step 4

Declare Your Career

There is nothing more liberating
and catalyzing than declaring.
—Anonymous

Often careers don't get off the launchpad due to analysis paralysis. For many it's easier and more enjoyable to think about career possibilities and not lock themselves into a specific career course. Doing so will simply ensure a life of unrealized potential and possibilities. Realizing career wealth requires you to make a career choice and commit to it. In this chapter you will take the fourth step in establishing your career foundation by declaring your career.

Clarifying Your Choice

When you have chosen your career work, you need to clarify and refine this choice with a career declaration. This is a note to yourself describing the direction you will take your career, and why. It can be as simple as a one-paragraph statement or as involved as a three-page description of career goals and rationales. Whatever the length, you will find that as you describe your career to yourself you will achieve even more clarity about your career direction. This is also a final check to yourself—if you don't get excited when writing your career declaration, you need to back up and reevaluate your career choice. Just thinking about your career choice and writing it in a career declaration should excite and energize you.

Once you have completed this career declaration, you will have established your career foundation. When completed with serious intent, this inner core of the Career Wealth Model will provide the self-discovery and insight needed for you to emerge with confidence and passion. As you venture down your chosen career path, the career declaration will be a constant source of energy and focus, and just as with Michael Dell and the host of others who have declared themselves, your declaration will set in motion a clear destiny. Over time, opportunities will emerge when you need them. When this deep choice is coupled with your use of the six navigating practices described in part 2, you will quickly mobilize your career and life—your organization will rally around and support the achievement of your career declaration.

The example below should help you to create your own career declaration in Discovery Exercise 10, which follows.

EXAMPLE
Career Declaration

My career work is to marry my passionate core needs of learning, teaching, creating/improving processes, and solving problems with my background in business-to-business sales and service. Specifically, I will work as a process consultant within organizations, focusing on applying process improvement tools to sales and service functions. I will learn about, develop, and teach cutting-edge process improvement tools tailored to the unique needs of these functions.

DISCOVERY EXERCISE 10
Your Career Declaration

Directions: In the space provided, create your career declaration by describing the work you will seek based on your passionate core needs (refer to your list of passionate core needs in Discovery Exercise 6, p. 61).

Once your career declaration is completed, you will likely feel renewed and experience a sense of energy and anticipation. Don't keep this energy bottled up. Instead, let it fuel all the practices in the outer band of the Career Wealth Model. Sharing your career declaration will liberate you and catalyze the people and events around you.

The Liberating Effects of a Career Declaration

You may find it difficult, even risky, to publicly declare your chosen career. Possibly you feel a public declaration commits you to a career course. Forever wanting to keep your options open, you may never clearly state and stick with your career declaration. Or, you may not want to tell your manager and other important people in your life because you are worried your choices will disappoint these people and possibly even put your job at risk.

Whatever your reason, keeping your career declaration hidden will subdue your spirit and strength and will ultimately lead to frustration. In this state it would have been better if you had not known what you love. Along with the enlightenment of knowing what you love comes the need, even responsibility, to let it out. So, declare it!

You will find that making your career declaration is an empowering experience. By taking this seemingly simple first step you will feel a sense of liberation, self-determination, and greater commitment to your career direction. You will feel that you are sharing the best part of yourself for the world to see. People who achieve sustained career wealth own their life and declare their life's work regardless of the opinions of those around them. They have learned the power of being completely open and transparent with their passions and intentions. Such was the case for a previous associate. Let's call him Ken.

KEN

Ken had wallowed for years not knowing what kind of career he really wanted. After taking an extra year to finish college, Ken hopped between three different jobs and careers in five years, never being totally fulfilled and comfortable with what he was doing. Six years after starting his postcollege professional career Ken identified his passionate core and developed a career declaration. He was excited by the clarity of his life's work, but he was nervous about sharing this with his manager, worrying that she might terminate him when she realized his career declaration had him moving into the information technology field and out of the recruiting job he held currently. Ken did not yet have a job in IT and financially could not go without working.

However, when his manager came to town, Ken couldn't be muzzled and he took the opportunity in their one-on-one review to share his career declaration. To his surprise, once the manager was assured that Ken would not leave immediately and would work with her on a transition plan, she went out of her way to help Ken move into an IT role in a different part of the company.

Another friend of ours we will call Dennis was extremely dissatisfied with his work in a factory.

DENNIS

Once Dennis identified his passionate core and made his career declaration, he realized that he needed to find an outdoor position that allowed greater freedom. When he went to work the next day, Dennis asked his supervisor to lay him off so he could use the three-week severance package to cover his living expenses while he found work he really wanted to do. His manager was impressed with his candor and clarity of direction, but instead of laying Dennis off, she asked him to be patient and they would see if they could find him a better role in the factory. Within a month Dennis was in a new position in the same company performing deliveries. He was no longer stuck inside and he had the freedom and autonomy he needed. Dennis and the company both came out as winners. Clearly, Dennis took a real risk to find alignment with his passionate core.

Declaring yourself is not a one-time event. It is something you will continue to do throughout your life. Indeed, you will feel a person can't really know you unless they know about your life's work. By constantly sharing your career declaration you will also help people to support you in doing your life's work.

The Catalyzing Effects of a Career Declaration

Joe Frodsham first bumped into this principle a decade ago. He has always been passionate about travel and discovering new places. Among other related activities he would watch TV programs about different parts of the world. One time he found an especially interesting program about the country of Belize. Joe was fascinated by the country's landscape, history, and people, and was excited by the recreational opportunities off its shores. During the week after seeing the show about Belize, he remembers, he talked to five different people about the country and all it had to offer the tourist.

In the following weeks, three of these five people called Joe to ask him more about Belize and where they should stay when they visited there. Each person had adopted Joe's passion for the country—one even assumed he had been there himself and another made Belize his honeymoon destination. Joe was amazed at the impact he had on these people—they were willing to spend thousands of dollars and dedicate their precious vacation days to travel to a country based almost solely on the passion he had expressed. He didn't really know much about the actual country; he'd never even been there. However, it wasn't Joe's deep understanding about the facts of Belize that caught their interest; it was his excitement about the country.

This experience led Joe to conduct more analysis and research. He found that often when he had shaped and influenced people's behavior it had been when he was passionate about something. Whether it was when as a teenager he had motivated his dentist to follow his passionate pursuit and begin a coin collection or as an adult when four friends asked to invest in a rolling stock portfolio he was excited about—these and similar examples led Joe to recognize that he was most persuasive when he was truly passionate about something, not when he was the most knowledgeable or when he was unnaturally trying to position or sell something.

A host of more empirical studies back up the role of personal beliefs and feelings in mobilizing others (see, for example, C. O. Word, M. P. Zanna, and J. Cooper, "The Nonverbal Meditation of Self-Fulfilling Prophecies in Interracial Interaction," *Journal of Experimental Psychology* 10, 1974). Each of these studies concludes that a person's emotions can't be hidden or contained. When people feel your positive energy and excitement, they don't want to douse the flames; instead they want to fan the flames and enjoy the heat. We are all attracted to positive emotions.

Time and again we have seen this principle demonstrated in the career context. When you make your career declaration, others instinctively try to help: the relative who tells you about a neighbor who is an expert in your desired field, the co-worker who tells you about an outside seminar you should go to, or the manager in the other department who needs someone to work on a project she knows you would love to be part of. As you continue to share your career declaration, others will help pave your career path with you.

This practice is so powerful it can sometimes lead to trouble. When you declare your career desires, people will want to help and be part of your success story. If your career desires are focused on a position instead of your life's work, beware. It may lead to getting roles that you know will make you happy but for which you may not be ready. Such was the case for a previous employee we will call Alison.

ALISON

Alison declared that she wanted to be a "vice president of anything." She wanted the big title. (We call this the "Title Syndrome"—focusing on organization level and status instead of your life's work.) She had declared this openly and often. People liked Alison and wanted to make her happy; when a leadership position in Marketing opened up, Alison was promoted to vice president and put in the role.

Everyone was pushing for Alison to be successful in this stretch role. Unfortunately, she stumbled repeatedly. A year into her new role everyone agreed that she was not working out, and she left the company. Both she and her previous employers learned to be more cautious and to be sure not to put people into positions they desired instead of positions for which they were truly ready.

In contrast to Alison's experience, if your career aspirations are based on your life's work as stated in your career declaration, you will likely avoid the pitfalls of merely acquiring the symbols of success offered by the organization and will not abdicate career control and passion to the whims of others. Indeed, focusing solely on "getting ahead" as defined by your organizational level is at the heart of a lot of organizational dysfunction and personal career stress. It is a contributing factor to misdeeds perpetrated by corporations such as Enron, Adelphia, and others as well as the pervasive phenomenon of the "Peter Principle," which describes

how time and again people are promoted to their level of incompe-
tence. These organizational and individual problems have a common contributing factor: people who are motivated by what they
want to have instead of what they love to do.

However, as you declare your life's work, you will mobilize a
network of support. People, ideas, and opportunities will emerge
directly as a result of the focus and energy generated by your
career declaration.

Your Declaration

It's time for you to declare. The people who are most important in
your life and career need to know first. They shouldn't learn from
others. It may be helpful to write down the names of people you
will tell initially and cross them off as you work through the list.
Over time such list making won't be necessary, as everyone will
know of your career declaration, and new people in your life
will soon learn of your passion for your life's work. Use Discovery
Exercise 11 for this purpose.

DISCOVERY EXERCISE 11
Declaring Your Career

Directions: In the space provided, record the names of people
you need to declare your career to.

-
-
-
-
-
-
-
-

Your Career Foundation . . .
A Final Note

Everyone who has conscientiously worked through the steps to establish their career foundation has had a powerful experience. For some it has surfaced feelings and passions that had been dormant for some time, while for others it has provided more clarity around what they already knew they loved, resulting in greater confidence and commitment to their current career choices. So, as you make this inner discovery, realize that you are taking time to ask yourself some questions that dig deeper than you normally go.

As you work through the steps to establish your career foundation, don't be surprised if this process surfaces powerful thoughts and feelings. This could generate a myriad of emotions, ranging from sadness to happiness to regret to a sense of elation. If and when you feel these emotions, don't push them away, as this is critical to your self-discovery and illustrates the necessity of this process in bringing you to a higher level of awareness and alignment around your passions. Instead, stop to consider what you are learning about yourself and your passions. We recommend that you study these feelings by talking to someone or writing in a journal. Then, once you feel you're ready, continue to step through the process. One thing is guaranteed—as you take the time to work conscientiously to establish your career foundation, it will change your life.

Such was the case with a colleague of ours we'll call Alan.

ALAN

Alan had built a successful career developing and leading sales organizations. At thirty-eight, Alan realized he was happy with his accomplishments and had achieved a secure place as a valuable member of his organization, but he longed to be doing something else. He found that he missed the excitement he had felt earlier in his career; however, when he shared these feelings of longing with friends and family they thought he was crazy and told him to be happy with what he had achieved and enjoy his status and job security.

*As Alan worked through the steps to establish his career
foundation, he realized that at his passionate core was a strong
need to be chasing a dream and to have a sense of self-determination, creating a unique path all his own. His current position
was secure, but he felt he had already achieved his dream and
taken all paths within his company. He thought he had nowhere
to go and nothing worth chasing where he was. Alan needed
a new dream to chase that allowed him maximum freedom.*

Based on this insight Alan considered quitting his job and
turning his efforts to chasing his dream of starting his own company in an emerging area of the packaging industry. However, in
the midst of planning to leave his company Alan took the time to
consider how he could possibly fulfill his core needs while staying
where he was. He enlisted some others in considering alternatives
and over a few weeks he defined a position the company did not
have but which Alan felt was needed—developing and executing
strategies to go after new market opportunities. Long story short,
Alan got agreement for this new position and became reenergized,
and is now having the time of his life. It's fun to be around Alan—
his excitement is contagious and he is finding success helping the
company expand aggressively into new markets. It really is a win-
win for Alan and his company. We are sure that he will continue
to find career wealth in this company as long as he stays aligned
with his passionate core. As example after example have shown,
people and rewards are attracted to the energy generated by people driven by their passions.

Finding and Leveraging
Your Passionate Core

We have shared our principles for career wealth, and you've read
the stories and examples for establishing your career foundation.
We hope you have also completed the personal application work.
If not, stop here and set aside the time to do that. The steps in this
first part of the book will be as powerful and transformative as
you make them.

SUMMARY

- Share your excitement. You are excited about your career declaration—don't keep it bottled up; share it with others.

- A career declaration is liberating—sharing your career declaration will provide you with a sense of release, direction, and freedom.

- A career declaration catalyzes people around you—the energy from your career declaration will be contagious; people will be attracted to your excitement and will want to help.

- You need to declare your career—go forth and share . . .

Part 2

Your Career

Navigation

Six Practices for Taking the Inside Out

Destiny is not a matter of chance, but a matter of choice.
It is not a thing to be waited for. It is a thing to be achieved.
—William Jennings Bryan

In part 1, "Your Career Foundation," you completed a process for setting the foundation for your career by uncovering your passionate core and defining your life's work. This inner awareness and commitment to a career choice is deeply personal work that draws fully upon the passionate core needs that are uniquely yours. You likely now have greater career direction and energy than you have ever experienced. This passion is essential to having a healthy and successful career; however, it is not enough. In fact, it could lead to greater frustration. Let us explain.

Career frustration can arise when you understand your passionate core but are not able to express it in your work. Time and again we see people disenchanted with their career, chronically upset by the fact that their manager or the organization underappreciates them and does not see the value they can add or are adding. These people know what they want to do and how it could benefit the organization, but they don't know how to get the organization to support and reward their passions.

Some try to do what they love in an organization by going out of their way to get noticed or to sell themselves. However, these self-promotion efforts are about "self-branding," which generally seems fake, often annoys people, and rarely has the intended effect. Some get upset by having to "play politics," as if considering the social dynamics of an organization in the course of their work is somehow beneath them or requires them to significantly compromise their values and passions.

The Six Practices of Career Navigation

Part 2 focuses on navigating your career context, both the stated and unstated rules you need to know to be supported and rewarded in your career. The rules are different in each organization, but the practices necessary for navigating are the same:

- **Practice 1:** Shape Your Role—build your perfect role

- **Practice 2:** Be the Players—make key decision makers your champion

- **Practice 3:** Get Equipped—develop your capabilities

- **Practice 4:** Know the Road Rules—follow your company's real rules for success

- **Practice 5:** Network—surface opportunities through your connections

- **Practice 6:** Check In—stay connected with your passionate core

People who have consciously or instinctively learned and applied these practices are continually rewarded and constantly embraced by their organization. Adopting any one of them will be highly beneficial. These six simple yet powerful practices are

Figure 4: The Career Wealth Model

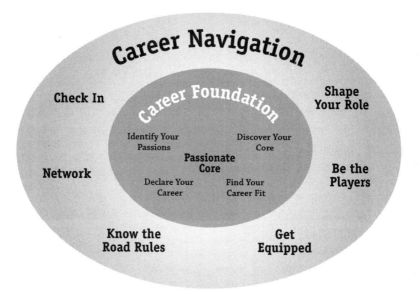

Career Navigation

Check In

Shape Your Role

Career Foundation

Identify Your Passions

Discover Your Core

Passionate Core

Network

Declare Your Career

Find Your Career Fit

Be the Players

Know the Road Rules

Get Equipped

included in the outer band, "Career Navigation," of the Career Wealth Model (repeated in figure 4).

Remember that real career wealth starts on the inside—these six navigating practices are especially powerful when aligned with your passionate core. Then they become the means of getting the world to support what you love. Inversely, if you have not done the inner core work first, there is a high probability that you will use these practices to acquire organization recognition and power for their own sake. In this case it is your lust for the symbols of success that is driving your career decisions, and although these practices may serve you well in the short term, you will never realize the fulfillment of truly doing what you love. Later on you will likely feel a sense of quiet desperation—even though you are being treated well by your organization you will still not be fulfilled in your work. We've seen many people sadly wearing these "golden handcuffs" who, despite the career progress and security they have achieved in their organization, feel unfulfilled. These people are attached to the organization because of the outward trappings of success but have not identified and aligned with their passionate core.

Throughout part 2 we describe each of the six practices of career navigation. The order in which they are presented or studied is not important; there is no required sequence, as the practices don't build on each other. Instead, these are practices to be used regularly and concurrently.

Once you make a clear and deep choice to do what you love, unconventional circumstances, people, and opportunities will present themselves. Trust your instincts and expect opportunities you could not have imagined to emerge. When this happens, be prepared to use the six practices of career navigation.

Have fun navigating your career!

Practice 1

Shape Your Role

Man stands in his own shadow and wonders why it's dark.
—Zen saying

Almost every organization has job descriptions and performance reviews. These documents provide the organization with a sense of role alignment and predictability, and provide each employee with role clarity. People find these documents so important that they often complain if they don't have a current job description and performance review. Some consider the absence of these documents as clear evidence of bad management. It's clear that most people want clarity and predictability in their job.

Effectively navigating your career in alignment with your passionate core often requires that you look beyond available roles. In practice 1 you will learn how to build and shape your perfect role in your organization.

You Are Not Your Role

Job descriptions and performance reviews overall are a good thing; however, they can actually stifle opportunities if they are treated as the complete, immutable description of what an employee should and should not do. Every role in an organization is dynamic. Tasks and objectives change based on business necessity, expectations of management, and the capabilities and passions of the incumbent. However, most job descriptions and performance reviews are static; they don't change along with the changing needs and personalities of an organization. As a result, they soon become dated and/or ambiguous documents that put employees in a box. The fact is, those who wrote your job description, or even performance review, likely never had your job—at least the way it is currently configured. They don't know the demands and opportunities of the position today as you do. And they have no way of knowing your unique passions and how they can be leveraged on behalf of the organization.

People and managers in your organization don't know what they don't know. The very rational process of defining a job description assumes that a manager knows what a person in a role should be doing before he does. As a person in a role with a job description and set of performance objectives, you should not put too much stock in it. To be clear: You are not your role as defined by someone else—you should not feel confined by how your role is described on a piece of paper.

Looking Outside Your Box

The real opportunities in your organization are likely in the space between roles. These are the opportunities you and others see that nobody else is chasing, or the things you would love to do but haven't taken the time or risk to do. It is in these spaces outside your defined role that you can find the opportunities to do what you love at work. And as you do what you love, people will be attracted to you and your organization will support and reward you. People in your organization don't know that they want, even need, the work you love until they see you do it. So, show it to them. As you do, any new job description or performance review you get will include what you love to do.

Shandra is an example of someone who found an opportunity outside her position.

SHANDRA

At her passionate core Shandra needed to communicate, to teach, and to convey stories and information in a unique, compelling way. One of her resulting passions was creating home videos.

One day, while discussing the lack of consistent and effective communication from senior management in her company, she had an idea. She felt there was an opportunity to create and distribute videos of messages from senior leaders to help promote communications throughout the company. This wasn't part of her job description. However, she wrote a one-page proposal and sold her manager on giving it a try in their relatively small information technology group (three hundred global employees). Shandra used her own camcorder to tape her boss and on her own time consulted with outside professionals on how to get the sound and graphics just right.

Shandra's video was very well received, and her manager gave her a small budget to produce and distribute a new video every quarter. As she got better at video production, the organization's awareness of her work grew. Her work became so highly regarded that within two-and-a-half years of her initial video she was running a small video production group in the company. Shandra and her team of two were responsible for facilitating strategic internal communications via multimedia solutions such as videoconferencing. Despite the number of company layoffs in the years since, Shandra and her group have never lost their funding. They have become an integral, even strategically important element of the deployment of the strategy. Shandra herself has taken on additional management responsibilities over her company's intranet and leadership events. She has also become well known for her work outside the company and is regularly offered job opportunities at other companies. All this started with Shandra finding a space to express her passion in her organization.

In Shandra, we see a person who looked completely outside her role to find expression for her passionate core. Video production was not one of her stronger skills when she started. However, she went from dreaming to doing. Shandra's case is similar to that of all who step out and do what they love. It doesn't matter if they are skilled or not, or even if their passion makes sense. Just like Shandra's manager did for her, others will see the gleam in your eye and want to support your efforts.

Are there spaces and opportunities outside your position to express your passionate core needs? Sometimes aligning with your passions may simply mean expanding your current role. Such was the case of a marketing professional we will call Jason.

JASON

At his passionate core Jason needed to learn, synthesize information, and create new theories and approaches. For this reason he had long fantasized about being a professor with the freedom to learn and hypothesize. However, after he completed the Career Wealth Indicator (see Discovery Exercise 1) and uncovered his passionate core, it was clear that all his passionate core needs were finding expression in his current role except for his need to create new theories. After Jason reviewed his career options using the Career Risk and Alignment Tool in Discovery Exercise 9, he felt his best option was to look for opportunities related to his role as a competitive intelligence manager.

In this role, Jason and his group were constantly scanning the competitive environment, deciding which information was important and then passing on the information to senior leadership and strategy and sales groups in his computer hardware company. Jason decided to put his passionate core to good use and, instead of simply handing off the information to other people, he started providing an interpretation of the data. His

*interpretation spotlighted trends, connected seemingly unre-
lated facts, brought in marketing and economic theories to
help explain the data, and made projections. Jason called his
expanded work the "Blue Report." It was a risk for him, as this
type of analysis and projection generally came from a senior
leader in the strategy group, not a manager in competitive
intelligence. He had informed his manager before he sent the
first Blue Report. His manager had seemed curious and said
somewhat skeptically, "We'll see how your report is received."*

*Jason's first Blue Report took some people by surprise, but
overall it was well received. Most deemed it to be better reading than the simple numbers and summaries sent previously,
and although some in the strategy group disagreed with
his theory and projections, they at least read and took his
input seriously. Based on this kind of feedback, future issues
of Jason's Blue Report evolved, with some sections being
added and others deleted. Happily, over time the Blue Report
became a highly anticipated read for many throughout the
organization and it fostered broader strategic discussion than
ever before. And, Jason was more passionate about his role
than ever.*

Jason's experience has been repeated many times. As people
step out and do what they love in their organization, they find
acceptance. Their initial step is often tentative, deemed to be a
risk by their colleagues and managers. However, inasmuch as their
work comes from their passionate core, it appears genuine and
people are attracted to it. The fact is that the roles or boxes that
constrain us do so only because we allow them to. It is those who
step out who are recognized and rewarded over time. Organization
leaders often wish that their employees would step out of their
box. It seems that many employees perceive there are more constraints to following their passions than really exist. Whatever the
attitude of your managers, they would be energized by your passions and would not only allow, but likely go out of their way to
support, your doing what you love. Remember, most constraints
to realizing your career declaration are self-imposed. Once you

discover what you love, you can find the space and freedom to make it happen.

Taking Control

Shaping your role in an organization is at the source of taking control of your career. It puts you in the driver's seat and distances you from the vast majority of employees who simply wait for the organization to hand them a role. It should not be surprising that employees abdicate their power to their organization. Most of us spend our formative years, as children and adolescents, in formal schools, where we are taught to sit up straight, follow the rules, and conform. We are taught to stay within certain boundaries, and this lesson lasts into our professional work life. Unlearning this lesson can feel awkward, even wrong at times. But remember, it is not wrong to do what you love; in fact, it is the best way you can serve the needs of your organization.

Four Steps for Shaping Your Role

As you shape your role, make a conscious effort to use the other five practices of career navigation as well. You'll find that your loves and the needs of the organization will begin to converge in unique ways. Below is a four-step process for shaping your role within your organization in this manner. This process will enable you to act instead of merely waiting for a job to open up that you can apply for.

1. Define your perfect role. Using your career declaration as a guide, think about the kind of work you love to do; in other words, your perfect role. In defining your perfect role, start with a blank slate and forget what roles are available in your current organization. Then, ask yourself, "What would my perfect role look like?"

In answering this question, deploy the power of visualization. Take some time to picture what you would be doing in a perfect day, week, and month. Visualizing your perfect role is not simply an enjoyable thing to do. Focusing your mind and heart generates incredible power. All successful creators—whether they are performers, athletes, designers, trainers, or businesspeople—rely on active visualization to shape, create, and achieve. California Governor Arnold Schwarzenegger, for example, used the power of visualization to achieve multiple Mr. Universe titles. Before each weightlifting session he would visualize each muscle as he wanted it to be. Seeing your career is the first creation.

In many workshops we have illustrated the power of visualization by having two groups perform the same task, the only difference being that one group visualized successful completion of the task before performing it. The group that visualizes always performs significantly better. You should foster this capability of visualizing. It starts by creating your perfect role in your mind. Be clear and specific about those elements of the work that are important to you and your career declaration.

Once you have visualized your perfect role, document it in a role description, which should include

- Role objectives

- Key groups and customers you will work with

- Additional unique characteristics of the role (hours, location, and so on.)

Writing the description may take a while—hours or even a whole day—and it is not completed until you have clearly defined one absolutely excellent role for yourself. Once the task is completed you will have energy that is now very focused. You will know in great detail what the role looks like. Now it's a matter of going out and getting it. To be clear, this perfect role is dynamic. You are never locked into a role but instead can visualize different roles and change if and when you wish.

If your perfect role description happens to be your current role, then you can return to your position with a renewed sense of commitment. However, it may be that achieving your perfect role will require you to extend your current role or shape a totally new one.

2. Do your homework. With the description of your perfect role in hand, it's now time for you to do some research. Specifically, you need to find out where your role would best fit in your organization. This may be obvious—if it is, move ahead to step 3. If it is not obvious, answer the following questions:

- Is my perfect role the same as or similar to a current role in my organization? Where is this role?

- If my perfect role is not similar to an existing role in my organization, in what department or area would it find a home? Where could it add the most value?

Answering these questions may require you to talk to people with more information, possibly people you don't know personally. As you do, you will find that people will be open to helping you understand their part of their organization and helping you to understand the roles and opportunities.

These questions will generate some ideas and options. It's important to consider all the information and identify where in the organization your perfect role would best fit—both for you and for the people in your organization. In other words, think of where you could have the biggest impact and how it would affect the people and your organization in the most positive way. Not only is this the right thing to do, it will also help you influence people to shape and sustain this role in your organization. Once you have clarified where in the organization you need to be, you will be ready to begin shaping your perfect role in steps 3 and 4.

3. Influence the players. As discussed in the first chapter, organizations are simply a collection of people, and because of that, decisions in organizations are not always rational. Instead, as we discuss later in practice 5, "Network," it's not just what you know and want, it's also who knows and wants you. Achieving your perfect role requires you to use practice 3, "Be the Players," to identify the people you need to influence to shape your role. The players could include any number of people. It could be your manager who can approve a simple expansion of your current role, or it could be people and groups who need to believe in the possibilities of the new role you want to shape. When going through this process, be courageous and remember that the key leaders and groups you are influencing are simply people who will be engaged by your passion.

Try to look at yourself the way others see you—assume the "view from the balcony." Don't get so focused on the role you are in and what you want that you fail to understand other perspectives and appreciate how your desired role would affect others in your organization.

4. Be patient, be observant. Once you know what you love and want, it can be difficult to be patient. It is easy to get frustrated and even cynical when others don't do what you want or react quickly to what appears to be in the best interest of everyone. When this happens, remember that it is a career, not a job. Shaping your life's work is rarely a quick process. Be braced for the fact that it may take a while—weeks, months, even a year or more—to shape your perfect role. In this process use all the elements of the "Career Navigation" band and don't give up—both conventional and unconventional things will happen to enable you to move into your perfect role. And, when the opportunities present themselves, pounce!

The story of a colleague we will call Kim illustrates how to be patient and observant.

KIM _____

Upon turning forty, Kim took some time to figure out what he wanted in the rest of his career. He uncovered his passionate core needs and developed a career declaration. In shaping his perfect role he saw himself leading a small performance consulting group in his organization. At the time there was no performance consulting group in the company, and as a human resources director he had never managed an internal consulting group before.

Kim did all the right things to shape his perfect role. He did his homework and met with and shaped the thinking of key stakeholders. And he generated a lot of support as people felt his enthusiasm and saw the possibilities of a performance consulting group in the organization. However, after five months, Kim was still in his HR director role and there appeared to be little progress made in shaping his perfect role. In fact, with the downsizing his organization was going through, Kim was being asked to do more than ever. Organizational resources were stretched, and there was little desire to add more headcount in the form of a performance consulting group. Kim felt he never would be able to shape his role in his company.

At this time Kim attended a meeting with one of his key players, the head of the regional business unit his HR group supported. In the meeting the regional leader discussed his concerns about the organization after the downsizing was completed. He was worried about the integration of the "right-sized" organization and all the cross-functional issues that needed to be managed after the new organization was formed. Seeing an opportunity, Kim reminded the leader of the performance consulting group concept and discussed the possibility of having a group like this focus for one year on new organization issues. To the leader and all others in attendance this seemed like a sensible, even obvious, solution. With the sponsorship of the regional leader, Kim was able to easily influence the global human resources head and organize a performance consulting group.

In retrospect, Kim realized that if he had not conceived of the performance consulting group five months before this meeting, he would not have thought of it as a solution to deal with downsizing issues. He also realized that had he taken the view from the balcony and not assumed the role of victim, he would have seen this possibility earlier.

For Joe Frodsham, looking outside his box allowed him to realize a fulfilling career. As he began chasing and embracing passions and opportunities within his organization and outside his role, he met new people, gained lots of support and exposure to the most senior leaders, and felt unencumbered. Earlier in his career he had spent about 90 percent of his time doing what he was supposed to do, staying within the confines of his role—all along feeling constrained and sometimes resentful. Once he started pursuing his passions by shaping his role and finding completely different spaces between roles, he found himself spending his time doing what he was passionate about. At times it was controversial, as he didn't always do what people expected, but overall he has been highly rewarded and supported by the organizations he has worked for—much more so than if he had stayed in the boxes he was placed in initially.

Studying the example below will help prepare you to work through all steps of practice 2 as you complete Discovery Exercise 12, which follows.

EXAMPLE

Shaping Your Role

What would your perfect role look like?

I see myself . . .

- Having time to research and refine typical process improvement tools and methods to apply to sales and service functions. I am working directly with senior leaders of the sales and service groups in our organization in the areas that have the biggest impact on the business and are in the most need of improvement.

- Having lots of flexibility in choosing which projects I work on. I am working on multiple (3–7) projects at any given time. However, I will be required to report the financial impact of my process improvements on a regular basis to ensure that my work is valued and sustained by the organization.

(cont'd)

EXAMPLE CONT'D

Shaping Your Role

What would your perfect role look like?

I see myself . . .

- Partnering with people inside and outside my organization as the demands and needs of each project dictate. However, I do not see myself managing a large group of people full-time. I will be a high-level technical specialist.
- Adding to the knowledge and understanding of my field. I accomplish this through conferences, in which I learn and also present to others in my field.
- As a roving expert in my company. And I see myself loving it!

Role Description

Role objectives:

- Annually, add over a million dollars in cost savings toward the financial performance of the company through the application of cutting-edge process improvement tools in the sales and services functions
- Improve the efficiency and effectiveness of the sales and services organizations around key performance metrics (e.g., employee morale, turnover, sales call effectiveness)
- Be a strategic resource for executives in driving the priorities of their sales and services organization
- Combine the expertise of an outside expert with the organization savvy and knowledge of an internal employee

Key groups and customers:

- Sales and services executives. They need to know me, direct me to the important projects, and sponsor this work.

EXAMPLE CONT'D

- Sales and services employees. They need to accept me, not see my work as a threat, and use the process and tools I introduce to help them and the company perform better.
- Process improvement associations and groups. I need to be an active member who participates actively in learning and networking.

Additional unique characteristics of the role:
- I have an office but do not have to be in my office—I have total flexibility to work out of my home when I am not traveling to a site.

When you have explored the opportunities within your company for defining and shaping your desired role, move ahead to Discovery Exercise 12

DISCOVERY EXERCISE 12
Shaping Your Role

Directions: Answer the question "What would my perfect role look like?" Visualize your perfect role and record it in the space below. Then create your role description by providing the role objectives, key groups and customers, and additional unique characteristics.

_____

_____

_____

_____

_____

(cont'd)

DISCOVERY EXERCISE 12 CONT'D

Role Description

Role objectives:

-
-
-
-
-
-

Key groups and customers:

-
-
-
-

Additional unique characteristics of the role:

-
-
-
-

SUMMARY

- You are not your role—the box you may feel is imposed on you is of your own creation, so look outside your box. This is the essence of taking control of your career.

- Shape your role—your opportunity to drive your passions and live your career declaration may require you to expand your current role or shape a new one.

- The four steps for shaping your role are

  1. Define your perfect role

  2. Do your homework

  3. Influence the players

  4. Be patient, be observant

Practice 2

Be the Players

We control 50 percent of a relationship.
We influence 100 percent of it.
—Anonymous

Essentially organizations are a collection of people focused on a common objective. To be successful within an organization, you must become adept at working with and influencing these people. They present your biggest trials but your greatest opportunities as well. Working with the tangible aspects of your job—technology, systems, and processes—is comparatively easy. Indeed, when Joe Frodsham was a consultant, the problem of every group he was brought in to help had as its root cause damaged trust and ineffective relationships among key people. It is the softer, or people, side of the organization that is really difficult after all and requires continual focus and attention.

In practice 2 you will proceed through a process for influencing the key decision makers who can determine your success.

People, Not "People Skills"

Literally thousands of books and seminars teach "people skills." These offerings run the gamut from developing presentation and negotiation skills to creating more active listeners. Almost all these offerings are based on the premise that communicating in a more polished way will help you work better with people and get better results through them. Building better communication skills is a good thing; it can help people become better at things such as presenting, negotiating, and listening. However, these offerings and techniques are minimally effective when it comes to being able to truly understand and influence key people in the organization. And to be clear, when it comes to shaping your role, there are key people you will need to influence. We call these people who are key to your career and your life in the organization *players*.

Those who find sustained success in organizations represent all styles and communication approaches. Indeed, many of the people cited as examples in this book don't have tremendous people skills. They may talk too much, not talk enough, or tell bad jokes. Gaps in their communication and people skills are open for the world to see. It would be a good idea for them (and for you) to reduce these gaps, but in fact these are not at the heart of the ability to influence others and shape opinions. In fact, exceptional communication skills can actually hinder one's ability to influence others as they may appear insincere or too slick. For example, Republicans in the 1992 presidential election derided Bill Clinton for his strong communication skills, calling him "Slick Willie."

So, if it's not a specific style or set of polished communication skills that provides this needed influencing capability, what is it? Quite simply, people who are able to effectively influence others and shape opinions are often those who are able to suspend their own perspective, even their own deeply held beliefs. This doesn't mean they give up their perspective, or necessarily adopt someone else's belief system. Instead, they realize that suspending their beliefs long enough to understand someone else's is necessary to influence others and shape opinions.

Perspectives

We all have our own perspective as typified by our unique ideas, approaches, and beliefs. This perspective shapes our world, but when it is not shared by those important to us (managers, employees, colleagues), it can cause conflict, hard feelings, and lots of frustration. Every day people share their perspective when they state their opinions about other people. When they tell you things like your employee is too quiet, your manager is too loud, or you are too distant, they are really telling you volumes about their own perspective. Truly, when people make an observation or provide feedback on someone else, the substance of their feedback states more about them—the person sharing the opinion—than the person they are talking about.

Having a perspective is not bad. Having a predictable set of ideas and beliefs is necessary to sift through and evaluate all the information that comes at you every day. Your perspective also drives a predictable set of behaviors so that people know how to effectively and comfortably interact with you. However, when you get stuck in your own perspective and are not able or willing to understand the perspective of someone else, you lose your ability to influence that person. Instead, by clinging to and solely championing your own perspective you cause conflict with and closed behavior from those you are trying to influence. Bottom line, to influence others, you must understand their perspective fully. That doesn't mean you need to adopt it.

Understanding another's perspective is not a new tactic. In fact, it is the basis of a lot of traditional interpersonal and communications training. Showing empathy, listening actively, and seeking first to understand others are all commonsensical and good rules to live by. However, there is a more powerful approach you can use to fully understand and influence another's perspective. It is an approach used by those relatively few who adeptly shape opinions and consistently have people support their agenda. For some of these people it is intuitive, so much second nature that they often don't know when they are doing it. And for others it is something they have consciously developed, although they may call it different things. We will call this approach the People Positioning Process.

The People Positioning Process

Joe first ran into the principles composing the People Positioning Process while working as a consultant. While staffed on some client engagements, he worked with an associate partner we will call Jenny.

JENNY AND JOE

Jenny appeared to have it all together. She was charismatic without being domineering, efficient without being impersonal, and incredibly effective at selling corporate consulting work. Everyone who worked with Jenny was engaged and excited, and always seemed to agree with her. We all felt we had a unique and special relationship with her.

As Joe got to know Jenny and what made her so effective at influencing people and shaping opinions, he learned that she had the very simple belief that all business success was ultimately based on relationships. Jenny believed that truly getting to know and appreciate others was the basis of being able to shape and influence them. As Joe got deeper into how she did this, he realized she not only sought to understand others, but she became the people *she was trying to influence.*

As we have worked with other rare characters like Jenny who are able to adjust to and effectively influence those they work with, we've seen that they all do a version of the same thing. They go beyond intellectually understanding another's perspective to truly feeling another person's perspective at a deep level. In essence, they become the person they are influencing. This is the People Positioning Process.

It may sound somewhat weird—even mystical—as if we were trying to have you project yourself into someone else and move into his or her body. In one way that is what we mean, but don't take it too literally.

Becoming the people you need to influence means that you adopt the fullness of their perspective for a short period. You visualize yourself in their position, feel the things they are feeling, think the things they are thinking, and experience the stresses they are experiencing. Then you look at yourself from their perspective and ask yourself, "What do I need from me?" The minute it takes for you to do this will result in a deeper understanding of people and bring with it clarity about what they need if they are going to be engaged and agreeable with you.

Embodying the people you need to influence is not intended to be manipulative, deceptive, or sneaky. People can feel when you are being disingenuous and insincere. Clearly over time, shallow, deceitful approaches will create more enemies than energy. Instead, by becoming another person you are understanding that person's position at a very deep level and using this understanding to better align his or her needs with your own. It is the optimal way to create win-win relationships.

The People Positioning Process is an incredibly productive and powerful way of aligning your needs with those of others. When coupled with a focus on bringing your passions and career declaration into your organization, it creates true champions, people who want to help you. Bringing this principle of becoming the people you need to influence effectively into your organization is achieved through the following three steps:

1. Identifying your key players

2. Being the players

3. Creating cause champions

Step 1: Identifying Your Key Players

In any quest within an organization you need the support of a few key people. Whether you are developing a new program, garnering resources to continue an initiative, or promoting a more comprehensive set of organization changes, their support is absolutely required. These individuals and groups are your key players. Similarly, in shaping your role, there are a few key players in your organization who must be on board and supportive. It may be your manager who needs to agree to changes to your role, the vice president who needs to agree to accepting a whole new type of role, or the technical steering committee who needs to approve resources for an experiment you want to lead. It's important to identify these critical players and categorize them as either level 1 or level 2 players:

- **Level 1** players are the two to four *key individuals* whose sponsorship is necessary for you to shape your role in the organization.

- **Level 2** players are the one or two *key groups* whose support is necessary for you to shape your new role in the organization. These are work groups, management teams, and/or steering committees that administer needed resources and/or provide required approvals.

When identifying the key players, you may be tempted to make a long and exhaustive list of people who are important in some way to you and the role you are shaping. However, on close examination you'll find that only a few real key players will make the decisions necessary to help shape your new role. Resist the temptation to include all stakeholders and keep your initial list and efforts focused on the critical few real players. And, after identifying these key players, document what you require of each. Reviewing the example below will help you to complete Discovery Exercise 13, which follows.

EXAMPLE

Identifying Your Key Players

Level 1 Players (Individuals):

Sandy, vice president, Sales: I need Sandy to accept my taking on the new role of process consultant in her organization. She needs to sponsor this role by ensuring that

---

her managers see it as a strategic priority and ensure that they consent to partner with me.

Charlie, function head of Six Sigma: I need Charlie to agree to expand the type of consulting his group sponsors and supports to include process improvement tools for the sales and marketing organization. I need him to be my mentor and guide as I develop the process consulting skills to augment my deep sales and marketing background.

Kerry, my current manager: I need Kerry to support my move into a process consulting role and allow me to spend time developing process consulting skills. When people contact him for a reference, Kerry needs to tell them that I have a strong passion for this new role and can help service, sales, and marketing groups in a unique way given my deep background in sales and marketing.

Level 2 Players (Groups):

Sales senior management group: Beyond Sandy's sponsorship I need each of her direct reports to recognize my value as a process consultant. I need them to surface projects for me to work on and help address resistance in the organization when it occurs. Essentially, I need each of them to be a tactical sponsor when I need it.

DISCOVERY EXERCISE 13
Identifying Your Key Players

Directions: Identify the level 1 and level 2 players and describe specifically why you need them.

Level 1 Players (Individuals):

-
-
-
-

Level 2 Players (Groups):

-
-

Step 2: Being the Players

As discussed previously, becoming the person you need to influence is at the heart of the People Positioning Process. Now that you have identified your key players, you need to take some time to become each key player. As you do so, you will gain insights about them (and yourself) that will be invaluable. You will be able to influence them in a way that aligns their needs with your needs and with the needs of the organization as well.

Being a key player begins by suspending your personal perspective, that is, your personal point of view, opinions, and biases. This is not easy, and, strictly speaking, it's almost impossible to recognize and suspend all of what you believe. But you need to go in and maintain an open mind and be willing to understand and not judge another person's position and perspective.

As you go through the process of being each of your level 1 players, you will gather invaluable information about the areas where you can serve as a solution for them by asking them specific questions. This will help you immensely in the next step as you persuasively make them your cause champion. You may find that you lack some data for one or more of the questions, especially if you don't know much about a key player beyond name and title. If this is true, ask those who do know the key player the same questions and any others that may help you get into his or her shoes.

You also need to ask these questions of your level 2 players. Given that these are groups of people, not individuals, you should choose one of the informal leaders of the group who typifies the experience and expectations of the rest. The samples below for both level 1 and level 2 players show the type of information you will want to gather. Due to space limitations, these samples are quite brief, but they will help you as you complete Discovery Exercise 14, which follows. In practice, you will likely gather much more extensive data, which will be incredibly useful as you go on to step 3 and create cause champions.

EXAMPLE
Being the Level 1 Players

Being Sandy, vice president, Sales:

What are my current priorities? Given that I was hired into this role three months ago, I am still trying to gain credibility with my staff and with senior leadership in the organization. I need a big win and have done some things that are different from, and exponentially better than, what my predecessor did.

Near the top of my list of priorities is supporting our disbursed sales group. We have to drive 10 percent sales and revenue increases year over year yet we are providing little in the way of additional resources and help for our sales group. They are feeling neglected and overworked—and, turnover in the group is too high. Another huge priority is establishing sales call effectiveness. Too many times we do all the work to get a salesperson in front of a corporate client and then we are not able to close the deal. Also on my priority list is the need to go global. We need to expand into neighboring markets such as Canada and, over time, Europe. I need to develop a strategy and support this expansion in the next year.

(cont'd)

What is causing me stress? I don't have enough time to do everything I need to do and I don't know who I can trust to delegate some of these important priorities to. Being new in the role, I don't have a great feel for the organization, what the important issues really are, and where the true leveraged opportunities lie. I have to reduce the hours I'm spending in the office and on the road—my family is being affected by my spending so much time away from home.

What are some significant changes I am experiencing? The biggest change is the new role itself. I have run sales and marketing organizations before, but not in such a large company, and I've never gone global before. Also, the culture of this company is different—it is much more intuitive and less planned than at my last company. This is okay; it just takes some getting used to.

How do I prefer to work and interact with others? I like a lot of detail. I hate grand statements and big ideas that aren't supported by good research or the numbers. I like people to send me the details and let me mull over them before a meeting. I tend to take my time in making decisions, but once the decision is made I want it implemented yesterday. I work hard and socialize little. Some people may consider me cold, but the people who know me know that I am very loyal. It just takes me a little while to warm up to someone.

What do I expect and need from you [insert your name] in order to take you and your career requests seriously? Prepare all your facts before meeting with me and show how the approach adds real value. Send me information before

---

EXAMPLE CONT'D

meeting with me and don't pressure me to make a quick
decision or see it your way. Time is important, so be efficient
and get to the bottom line quickly when we meet.

EXAMPLE
Being the Level 2 Players

Being a member of the Sales senior management group:

What are my current priorities? Achieving the monthly and
quarterly sales numbers is our ongoing number one priority.
A related priority is the attraction, development, and re-
tention of a highly skilled sales force. We need help in up-
grading our sales force capabilities. As we do this, it will
have an almost immediate impact on our sales numbers
and bottom-line performance. A third priority is better integration with the Product Development department. As the
people closest to customers, we need to help shape the next
line of products and services to meet the customers where
they are and where they're going.

What is causing me stress? The constant grind of achieving
ever-increasing sales quotas with no corresponding increase
in people and resources is difficult. You can get people to do
only so much before they leave the company for greener
pastures, which many of our good salespeople have done.
Clearly, if we keep doing what we've been doing, we will hit a
ceiling that will prevent us from increasing sales. This could
happen in the coming months.

(cont'd)

What are some significant changes I am experiencing?
We have a new manager, Sandy. She has been in her role for three months. Her style is very different from that of her predecessor. She is not very open and seems to be keeping her opinions to herself for now, so we're not sure what her agenda is and what changes she may want to make. Other than that, the interesting fact is that there is no change, and we need to change something fundamental in the sales organization to keep achieving the sales growth targets over the next few years.

How do I prefer to work and interact with others? We like to discuss things openly as a group. Basically, present an idea to us and let us discuss and debate it. In this way we get immersed in the idea and feel like we own it if and when it gets to implementation. If you simply impose something on us without facilitating our debate and involvement, it will probably fail. In addition, we like to look at possibilities. If you bog us down with too much detail around present realities, it will disengage us. We like to discuss and play with possibilities. I guess that's why we chose sales as a career. Finally, we are a bit territorial. If your proposal threatens our status or position, it will not be accepted.

What do I expect and need from you [insert your name] in order to take you and your career requests seriously?
Build rapport with us; don't just come to us and give your pitch. Who you are is as important as your ideas. We need to trust and like you as a person. Also, allow friendly debate; don't get hurt if we play devil's advocate. If you send us something to review prior to a meeting, make sure it's short and just covers the high-level benefits.

DISCOVERY EXERCISE 14
Being the Players (Levels 1 and 2)

Directions: Put yourself in the shoes of each of your level 1 and level 2 players per the instructions below. For level 2 players, choose one of the informal leaders of the group who typifies the experience and expectations of the rest. Record on individual copies of the exercise how you think each would respond to the specific questions below and other questions you'd like to ask.

For each player: Picture yourself in the player's position. Put yourself at her desk, with her manager, with her direct reports, and with all the unique characteristics of her person and position. Pay attention to the details around you as you visually put yourself in her situation, including the ambience, distractions, opportunities, and pressures. Once you are in her shoes, to the best of your ability answer the questions as if you were the player.

Name of level 1 player (individual): _____

What are my current priorities?

What is causing me stress?

What are some significant changes I am experiencing?

(cont'd)

How do I prefer to work and interact with others?

What do I expect and need from you [your name] in order to take you and your career requests seriously?

Name of level 2 player (group and group leader):

_____

What are my current priorities?

What is causing me stress?

What are some significant changes I am experiencing?

How do I prefer to work and interact with others?

What do I expect and need from you [your name] in order to take you and your career requests seriously?

Being the players is illuminating and even fun. However, if you stop and simply capture observations, you will not realize the power of the People Positioning Process. Applying your analysis to effectively shaping your role and the opinions of others happens in step 3.

Step 3: Creating Cause Champions

As people in organizations, we often find ourselves looking at other people and key players as impediments to what we want and love to do. At times we may even view these players as parents who won't let us do what we really want to do. In fact, much of the literature on influence and change is based on this assumption as it focuses on how to overcome resistance and surmount people like walls to be vaulted over. Those people who effectively influence others and shape opinions know this isn't true. They realize that the best strategy is not to change a person's opinion or go around or over them like hurdles. Instead, it is much more effective to approach people where they are. In other words, you will create cause champions if you make what is important to you important to your key players.

In doing this you are not attempting to change their perspective or what's important to them. Doing so will garner resistance 100 percent of the time, and you will be viewed as a nuisance. Instead, you will make what is important to you important to them if you *become their solution.*

Once you are a solution to their current issues, you have gone from trying to convince, work around, and/or go behind key players to having key players be your cause champions. These cause champions reach out to you to partner. They are the ones who will enable you to do what you love and to ensure that it will be sustained as you continue to be a successful solution for them and the organization. The work you create will also have a higher probability of being sustained even after you move out of the role, as it will be embraced as a solution by these important constituents.

The power of having cause champions is exemplified by a frustrated Web designer we will call Eric.

ERIC

*As a thirty-year-old Web designer, Eric went through the steps
to uncover his passionate core and develop a career declaration. In considering his perfect role, Eric saw himself developing cutting-edge and aesthetically attractive Web sites for his
company's intranet. This was a significant departure from the
role he had as a frontline supervisor in a large assembly plant.
However, determined to do what he loved, Eric got equipped by
learning a Web language and developed some prototype Web
pages and sites on his own time.*

*Eric's Web pages were attractive and had some very inter-
esting functionality, but when he showed the sites to his
manager and to people in other parts of his factory, they con-
gratulated him and nothing else. After two months of showing
everyone what he could do on the intranet site, Eric was dis-
couraged and even saddened. He was still a supervisor and no
closer to being the Web developer he wanted to be. It was clear
that people thought he did good work, but they didn't see how
his Web sites could support the operations in the plant.*

*Then, Eric took the next step and applied the People Posi-
tioning Process. As he did so he identified two level 1 stakeholders: Bruce, the corporate head of the group that ad-
ministered the company intranet; and Shane, the manager of
the small information technology group that kept the plant
systems running. He also identified one level 2 group, the operations management team that dealt with all day-to-day issues
throughout the plant. The process of identifying these critical
players was enlightening and allowed Eric to start focusing his
energies on influencing the critical few players through which
he could shape his new role.*

*As part of Eric's effort to step into the shoes of each level
1 and 2 player, he interviewed each one, asking them the
"Being the Players" questions with some follow-up probing
questions. At the end of this process, Eric knew that Bruce
needed more input from the factories to develop relevant Web
solutions; that Shane needed help selling his solutions to plant
supervisors who were behind the curve in using the informa-*

tion systems to do their job; and that the operations team was frustrated by the lack of accurate data needed to run the plant efficiently.

Finally, Eric went to each person and group of players and showed them how he could help solve their problems. As he did so, they became his cause champions, finding the funds and headcount replacement to allow him to move into his new role quickly. In his new role, Eric develops easy-to-use and intuitive Web pages based on the requirements of the supervisors on the floor and the information needs of the operations management team. He reports up to Bruce in the corporate group. This way Bruce and his group have a person in the field to test new Web tools they have developed, and the Web pages that Eric has created for his factory can be easily shared through the corporate group to sites all over the company.

Eric is an example and inspiration to all who want to shape a role in an organization. He went from supervising some employees in a plant to creating attractive and effective Web sites that were adding value throughout this large company. And, of course, he loved it.

Creating cause champions works. It is the way to bring your passions into your organization in a way that will get you supported and rewarded. To create cause champions in your organization, you need to use the analysis you did in step 2, "Being the Players," to identify the actions you will take to be the players' solution. Specific questions that need to be answered include these:

- How will the role I want to shape be a solution for the priorities and issues of these key players?

- How will I approach these key players to ensure that they fully absorb and buy into my solution?

This second question is especially important. Taking into consideration people's preferences for interacting with others will go a long way toward ensuring their understanding and buy-in. We've often seen silly style issues get in the way of key players' even considering a person's solution. In step 2 of the practice this is why we ask, "What do I expect and need from you [insert your name] in order to take you and your career requests seriously?" In the sample below, the different way in which Sandy and her management team are approached illustrates how style differences need to be taken into account. Reviewing these examples will help you as you complete Discovery Exercise 15, which follows.

EXAMPLE
Creating Cause Champions

Level 1 player: Sandy, vice president, Sales

How can the role you want to shape be a solution for the priorities and issues of this key player?

The process consulting role has to directly increase the capacity of the sales force without increasing budget or headcount. Sandy needs to see this as a means of increasing resources and building sales force effectiveness through process improvement. It also needs to be positioned as a breakout idea that Sandy is shaping and sponsoring. This is something different that she is seen bringing into the organization. The process consulting role also has to be positioned as making work easier for the sales force, not putting more demands on them. Sandy likes data, so I would try to ensure that sees me as a resource, sending real data and issues to be addressed from the field, bypassing the more subjective perceptions and biases she gets from those around her. She is stretched for time, so this role cannot be seen as something that she will need to manage actively.

The role needs to be seen as something that will save her time and support the growth of sales force capabilities. I need to develop a few scenarios that show the powerful savings and resource creation I can effect in this role.

Bottom line, my process consulting role is the answer to her need for sales force support, resource creation, and real data from the field.

How should you approach this key player to ensure that she fully understands and buys into your solution?

I need to send an introductory e-mail to Sandy and then leave her a short voice message introducing myself and indicating that I will schedule a thirty-minute meeting with her in the coming weeks. In the days prior to our meeting, I will forward a concise proposal to Sandy outlining the role of a process consultant in the sales organization and its benefits. I will include an outline of my background in sales and some references for her to check including my current manager.

Upon meeting with Sandy, I will respect her time and check that she has reviewed the proposal to see what additional detail I may need to add. I will let her control the conversation, but will ensure that at the end of the meeting she knows I am someone she should take very seriously. I will ask her what the next steps should be and make sure she knows this proposal is something she will be seen as driving.

(cont'd)

Creating Cause Champions

Level 2 player: Sales senior management group

How can the role you want to shape be a solution for the priorities and issues of this key group?

This team needs help and they are ready to embrace a new solution like the process consulting role. But it has to be something that will not be seen as a burden to the salespeople and will promote short-term wins that will help the group meet quarterly numbers. It can't be seen as a grand experiment, or as introducing a position that will be meddling in the affairs of the organization—I can't be Sandy's lackey.

This group is especially focused on making their sales force more capable and satisfied. I will need to be able to illustrate how I could improve people processes and positively affect things such as turnover and sales effectiveness. I need to reinforce my background in sales so they understand that I know their world. Like with Sandy, I need to develop a few scenarios that show the powerful savings and resource creation I can effect in this role.

How should you approach this key group to ensure that they fully understand and buy into your solution?

This role can't be seen as being imposed by Sandy, though Sandy needs to feel that this is her idea. There is some interesting tension that needs to be managed, which I will do by suggesting to Sandy that I meet each of her salespeople and review the idea with them. Given that she has a conservative nature and is still new and tentative with this group, Sandy will like this idea, as she can get their feedback through me. If they do like the idea, then she is seen as the sponsor and originator; if it is a bad idea, then it will have been "my" idea and she will be unscathed.

I will then set up a meeting with each member of the Sales senior management group. I will not send the proposal to them before the meeting—this would make it look like a final proposal. Instead, I will spend each meeting building trust by discussing who I am and allowing us time to get to know each other, and then reviewing the high-level elements of the proposal in an effort to solicit their maximum level of input. I will make sure that the unique feedback each member shares is included in what I review again with Sandy and what may go forward after that. They have to see themselves in whatever is ultimately presented.

DISCOVERY EXERCISE 15
Creating Cause Champions

Directions: For each of the level 1 and level 2 players you identified earlier, answer each question below in the space provided to help you begin to find the people who will champion your cause.

For level 1 players:
How can the role you want to shape be a solution for the priorities and issues of this key player?

How should you approach this key player to ensure that he or she fully understands and buys into your solution?

(cont'd)

DISCOVERY EXERCISE 15 CONT'D
Creating Cause Champions

For level 2 players:
How can the role you want to shape be a solution for the priorities and issues of this key group?

How should you approach this key group to ensure that they fully understand and buy into your solution?

Creating cause champions is not a complex process, but it is amazing how much more effective you will be with people as you apply the People Positioning Process. We caution that this is so powerful that it can be oversold. At times we have created cause champions that so value what we love to do, they can't get enough. Clearly, working with key players is an ongoing process as you continue to shape expectations, influence opinions, and also learn from their perspectives.

We recommend that you practice the three steps of the People Positioning Process with a friend, co-worker, and/or spouse. Treat them as you would a level 1 or 2 player; ask the questions and document how you could be a solution for them. As you test this with them you will learn the process, build a stronger bond and level of influence with the person, and learn a lot about yourself as you see yourself with their eyes. As you continue to use the People Positioning Process, you will find yourself applying it more informally as a matter of course in your daily interactions. Your overall level of adaptability to people and empathy for others will increase significantly. As coauthors, it has helped in our professional and personal relationships, especially in times of potential disagreement. It has been invaluable to put ourselves in each other's shoes and look back at ourselves from the other's perspective. Learning to use the People Positioning Process on the go like this takes some discipline, but it is immensely worth it.

SUMMARY

- **Success is about people, not "people skills"**—you don't need the most refined communication and people skills to work well with, and influence, people.

- **Don't get locked into your own perspective**—understand the perspective of the people you want to influence.

- **Become the people you need to influence**—view yourself from their perspective.

- **The People Positioning Process includes three steps:**

    1. Identifying your key players

    2. Being the players

    3. Creating cause champions

Practice 3

Get
Equipped

It usually takes me three weeks to prepare
a good impromptu speech.
—Mark Twain

You never get fully equipped; it's a lifelong process. To get equipped is to continually focus on acquiring the knowledge, skills, and resources needed to continually be performing your life's work. This includes training and access to people and ideas. It is making sure you have extended yourself into your life's work in such a way that you are always fully equipped to keep doing what you love.

In practice 3 you will learn to get equipped to realize your career declaration.

Within organizational settings people rarely take time to fully equip themselves. Things like mandatory training events are generally not aligned with their career passionate core, and they tend to avail themselves only of the people, ideas, and resources that immediately present themselves. Unfortunately, they are missing an excellent opportunity to use the organization's resources to more fully equip themselves to do what they love.

Achieving true career wealth requires you to take control of your career, often wresting it from the people and programs in your organization. Organization systems and processes are organized around achieving the needs of the organization, not your career fulfillment. However, with the direction and energy of your career declaration, you will put your relationship with the organization on more even ground as you more assertively pursue formal and informal opportunities to take training, meet people, and investigate opportunities that align with your career declaration. The advantage of being in an organization is that it provides you with people and resources you could never have access to independently. In this way your organization can truly support the achievement of your life's work. However, turning it upside down and having your organization rally around your career declaration requires you to understand how to equip yourself.

It's About Your Passions

Historically, education and development programs have focused on identifying and improving on people's areas of weakness, and on identifying and leveraging their areas of strength. As logical as this appears, it is the wrong focus. Your success and happiness in your career will have little to do with improving the things you don't do particularly well or even getting better at the things you already do well. Instead, your success and happiness will come from recognizing and leveraging your passions. Think about Michael Dell and Vincent Van Gogh, who will be known for their lasting creations, not their communication skills, and Bob Dylan, who will be remembered for his poetic lyrics, not his droning singing style. Similarly, you will not be known for your inabilities, but instead for the things you bring into being through your passion.

Instead of fitting into a box defined by the preconceived skills of your role, you will find extraordinary ways to add value by developing unique and deep skill sets in the area you are passionate about. So, if you have a passion for engineering, you should continue to learn and develop your capabilities in this field, even if you meet or exceed the organization's requirements for your role in this area. As your passion and unique skill sets meet, you will provide energy and competence that people will support and rally around. This will easily outshine all but the most serious weaknesses. It is this passion and brilliance that we often see in artists, performers, and sports stars. Perhaps that is why we look the other way and forget the often stormy, even dysfunctional, personal lives of some of these people.

Following our passions was a key learning for both of the co-authors. Some years ago, Joe Frodsham was a middle manager in a large company. In this role he went through a 360-degree assessment process in which his manager, peers, and direct reports provided him with feedback on a number of different leadership skills. The results in the feedback report showed a clear area for improvement: basic organization skills. In effect, there was a common perception that Joe didn't keep track of online and hard copy files and information very well. This report was quite accurate; he wasn't good at basic organization of the office area. When Joe considered how to address this area, it occurred to him that the solution would require him to spend lots of time creating and managing information and filing systems and take away some of the spontaneity and sense of freedom that he loved. Realizing that he needed to find a solution for the sake of his work group, together they finally found a process solution. One of Joe's employees who had a passion for managing details would take the minutes of each staff meeting and maintain a copy of all work and deliverables done by the group. As for the other aspect of his bad filing, they'd just have to learn to live with it. In this way they leveraged someone else's skills and passion to compensate for something Joe was not passionate about. One of his weaknesses was neutralized while someone else's passionate core was fulfilled.

So how do you get equipped to realize your passions? Begin by asking and answering the following simple questions: What are the tools, resources, and development you require to realize your passions . . . and by when will you require them?

Getting Equipped

Many formal and informal tools and resources have been designed to help you succeed within the realm of your career declaration. As you prepare a list of things you need to know and do in order to succeed, first consider who out there has been there before. Before you decide to reinvent the wheel, find out what others have done or are doing in your field of interest. Carefully select the areas you need to explore that support your career declaration, contact the appropriate organizations or people, and set up site visits or share information over the telephone. You will find that most organizations and people are proud of what they have accomplished and are willing to share their practices and success with others.

Top Ten Methods for Getting Equipped

Consider the following ten methods for supporting your career declaration:

1. Coaching. Performance coaching can be a very powerful tool to help you aggressively realize your success goals. Good coaching can set direction, create energy and focus, and help sustain momentum toward achieving desired goals. It is critical to find the right person to coach you for the right success criteria. It may be your manager, but not all managers are well equipped or desire to take on this role. If not your manager, then find someone who understands well what you are trying to accomplish and can be objective and firm about your progress along the way. Ensure that you meet regularly and establish clear success objectives and criteria you wish to be coached against.

2. Subject matter experts. There is no better place to gain valuable knowledge and information than directly from those who already have it. An organization typically is filled with thousands of experts in all kinds of disciplines and fields. Utilize the intelligence and experience of those around you. Seek them out and sit with them and ask them questions. They usually are very agreeable to helping.

3. Consultants. Although consultants can be expensive, they also can be very helpful in giving you an in-depth view and approach to a number of different subjects and disciplines. If you have aggressive time-bound objectives and a knowledge/experience gap, you may want to consider paying for an external consultant to assist you in getting equipped for success. This could translate into the transference of unique expertise and skills or perhaps provide an outsider perspective and counsel on key initiatives you are contemplating bringing in-house. Optimally consultants should be used to help and support rather than be relied on as the sole source of expertise or means of getting things done. Always be thinking about ways to minimize consultant usage and maximize the transference of their knowledge and skill as soon as possible.

4. Networks. This method is worthy of its own practice, hence practice 5,"Network." Imagine the power of an active body of people, flexible enough to help and support your informal information needs any time, all free of charge—that is the power of informal networks. The key to good networking is common focus and reciprocity. What can you give and what can you receive through identified people willing to stay in touch to help one another for a cause or common purpose? Perhaps your common purpose is information sharing in specialized areas such as finance, technology, and marketing. Or perhaps what's needed is a purge valve to the common stresses of daily organizational life. Select your networks carefully. Determine what you require from them and what you can give to them. Ensure that your networks have a common shared purpose and actively maintain them.

5. Societies and associations. Societies and associations can be very helpful. Most are formal and are organized around key areas of expertise or interest such as human resources, leadership, finance, and accounting. Societies and associations usually publish newsletters, create great learning forums on fresh topics, and have periodic meetings where members can make connections and build networks. Good associations can be an invaluable resource for getting equipped.

6. Mentoring. Mentoring typically is not about performance in a current role, but rather about capability in future roles. A good mentoring relationship must be founded on trust and enable open and transparent two-way conversation. The role of the mentor is to bring the broader perspective to the partnership and to act as a safe sounding board. Mentoring is not for everyone, but it can help you gain perspective and insight that otherwise might not be possible. If you aspire to continually grow and develop into broader roles with greater degrees of complexity, then you should consider mentoring as a resource. It is critical, however, that you be matched with the appropriate mentor—someone who truly has a valuable perspective to convey and with whom you are compatible.

7. Feedback. Every organization, group, and individual requires feedback to survive, learn, and grow. In getting equipped, both formal and informal feedback are needed to align you with your passions. Find out what formal feedback mechanisms are available to you and learn how to use them wisely. Coaching and mentoring are forms of feedback, as is a good 360-degree instrument completed by your boss, peers, and subordinates. Informal feedback mechanisms may also be available. You might appoint a monitor to keep an eye on you during meetings to tell you about critical thinking or behaviors you would like to change or improve. Typically, monitors are trusted colleagues at your level who will provide you with immediate and objective feedback.

8. Internal workshops and online learning. Check to see if your organization has an in-house learning and development curriculum. If so, there may be course offerings that could be useful to you in gaining the requisite knowledge and skills. For those organizations with limited in-class course offerings, you often will find online resources for getting equipped to achieve success in your role. These often include a full variety of online titles and courseware, many of which lead to formal certification. And of course there is the Internet. The World-Wide Web has a host of resources and information. Enter a few keywords in a search engine to begin your quest. Again, it is important to select those learning resources that will help you achieve focus and success. Do not waste your time, energy, and money on programs that will not specifically help you achieve your career declaration.

9. External workshops, seminars, and reading. These means of gaining knowledge and skills for your success are readily available—try to be selective. Before choosing, ask subject matter experts and those within your networks about the best books, periodicals, tapes, and seminars/workshops to check out. Otherwise you may find yourself in an overwhelming sea of information that will consume your time, energy, and attention with little return. Avoid becoming an "information junkie," and if a session is not adding the expected value, don't continue to waste your time; get up and leave. Life is short, so spend your time getting equipped around your passionate core!

10. Formal degrees and certifications. If getting equipped to complete your life's work requires you to get a formal degree or certification, review all your options before diving in. Because this is a major commitment, take the time to review program faculty and curriculum, references, cost, time to complete, and tuition assistance options. Take advantage of any tuition reimbursement your company offers along with financial assistance offered by other sources such as federal Pell Grants. Where there is the will, there is a way. We've known a number of people with little time or resources who have earned degrees and certifications. There is enough flexibility in programs and financing to make it happen if it is aligned with your passions.

Finally, you should continually equip yourself as you progress throughout your career. Ultimately any "getting equipped" list should be flexible and dynamic to accommodate changing realities and priorities.

Remember, you are in control of your career. Don't wait for your organization to identify the tools, resources, and development for you. These are things you must reach for and put into action. The application example below and Discovery Exercise 16, which follows, may help you get started in creating your own way of getting equipped.

You can use any or all of these four categories in completing Discovery Exercise 16.

EXAMPLE
Getting Equipped

What are the tools, resources, and development you require to realize your passions, and by when do you need them?

- **Formal degrees and certifications:**
- I need to get formally certified as a Six Sigma Black Belt in the next year

- **Mentoring:**
- In the next month I will find a Black Belt in the organization to mentor me
- In the next month I will find an external process consultant who is focused on sales and service processes to mentor me

- **Reading:**
- In the next week and on an ongoing basis I will scan the Internet and ask people for input on seminal articles and books to read in the area of process consulting

- **Societies and associations/networks:**
- In the next two weeks and on an ongoing basis I will join process consulting societies and forums and be an active member; this will set the basis for my network

---

Getting Equipped

Directions: Record your notes for becoming prepared in the space provided. Consider any of the categories listed earlier and add others you feel will be helpful to you.

What are the tools, resources, and development you require to realize your passions, and by when do you need them?

-
-
-
-
-
-
-
-
-

SUMMARY

- Get equipped by acquiring the skills, knowledge, and resources to do what you love continually.

- It's about your passions, not your strengths or weaknesses.

- The top ten list of methods for getting equipped is as follows:

  1. Coaching
  2. Subject matter experts
  3. Consultants
  4. Networks
  5. Societies and associations
  6. Mentoring
  7. Feedback
  8. Internal workshops and online learning
  9. External workshops, seminars, and reading
  10. Formal degrees and certifications

Practice 4

Know the
Road Rules

*Every company has two organizational structures: The formal
one is written on the charts; the other one is the everyday
relationship of the men and women in the organization.*
—Harold S. Geneen

Throughout the country, most people at some point in their late
teenage or early adult years learn to drive a car. This is usually a
long-anticipated event with parents watching with great trepida-
tion. Drivers-in-training get their initial direction from a parent,
friend, or driving teacher, and for the first few times they feel a little awkward behind the wheel. They don't know exactly what
speed to travel, and they wait too long or are too anxious at four-
way stops. Not having an experienced feel for the traffic around
them, they get nervous when they have to make a quick decision
about whether to stop or drive through a yellow light. It's a miracle
most of us make it through these early driving years relatively
unscathed.

As we become more experienced drivers, our comfort with the road increases. We are no longer as tentative and even become confident enough to multitask—simultaneously driving, finding a radio station, and talking on a cell phone. When we reach this point of comfort with driving, we have an intuitive feel for the road and the traffic around us. In the process, we follow many written and unwritten rules of the road. In fact, a lot of our driving behavior is dictated by a combination of written and unwritten rules, regarding such matters as

- **Speed.** In many places going the speed limit on a freeway could get you lots of honks and stares from passing motorists, but we all quickly slow to the speed limit when we see a patrol car.

- **Tailgating.** There is a safe distance to maintain between your car and the car in front of you, and then there is the much shorter distance maintained on many freeways and highways.

- **Switching lanes.** The required number of shoulder checks and amount of signal light time are rarely recognized on freeways and highways; instead, we charge to openings in our quest to be in the fastest lane.

Due to the many unwritten rules of driving, you can never really learn how to drive effectively by simply taking lessons and passing a written driving test. Instead, you need to drive the roads yourself, see what works for other motorists, and sometimes pay a ticket or get yelled at by another motorist when you stray beyond the written and unwritten rules of the road. Yet, once you have achieved confidence in your ability to drive, it can all be dashed when you drive in a different part of the country or the world, whether you're used to driving in a small town and find yourself competing with cabbies in Manhattan, driving a car in England on the left side of the road for the first time, or dealing with the crush of snarled traffic in Bangkok, Thailand. Different regions have different road rules you need to learn to navigate in order to drive safely. And until you learn them, the road can be frustrating and even dangerous.

In practice 4 you will learn how to effectively navigate the written and unwritten rules in your organization.

Beyond the road, written and unwritten rules exist in every social structure. Your family, community group, network of close friends, and organization all have a set of written and unwritten rules for interacting and working together. The written and unwritten rules in organizations are called many things: corporate culture, organization personality, company personality, corporate values, company DNA, and so on. These constructs all describe the same thing: the group's rules for working with each other.

The Road Rules in Your Organization

These written and unwritten rules are important. They create predictability and allow us to know what to expect when working with people in a social unit such as an organization. And as someone who wants to shape a role and do what you love in your organization, you need to know the road rules. In fact, with all the literature on organization culture, corporate values, and more, you may think you need to be an expert in how organizations evolve and why your organization does what it does. You may choose to spend a lot of time at this, but it's not really necessary in order to do what you love in your organization.

Just as driving your car does not require you to know exactly how a motor works or how the battery powers your vehicle's electrical components, you don't need to know all the reasons for how and why your organization does what it does in order to effectively navigate your organization. But, you do need to know the basic rules of the road in your organization, as it is these rules that will propel you or limit you. Above your organization's strategy, direction, or espoused values, these road rules dictate how things really get done.

Basically, these rules are a reflection of what people in your organization have consistently been rewarded for and what they have consistently been punished for. Over time, this has reinforced a set of behaviors that is constant across groups, units, and to some degree the whole organization. These behaviors are reinforced by the stories in your organization. The next time you hear about one of your corporate legends, listen to what made that person a hero or a victim. What rules of the road did he or she uphold or violate?

As an organization matures, people in the organization establish homeostasis, or a predictable and set way of behaving with and around each other. This set way of doing things becomes very entrenched and difficult to change. In fact, people want so much to maintain the steady state, they will often unknowingly resist any attempt to drastically change routine behaviors, even overtly working around new systems and processes meant to change the rules of the road.

And to be clear, your organization is probably trying to change or shape these rules. The may call it a "cultural change." In this effort to redefine the road rules, you may see written mission statements, corporate values, the company story, and even company philosophy statements. These written rules are important to know. You also need to know that to one degree or another they may not reflect the real rules of the road—just as the "65 MPH" speed sign on the New Jersey Turnpike does not reflect the average commuting speed of 81 mph.

Navigating the Rules in Your Organization

Once the rules in your organization have been established, they are very hard to change. In fact, senior leaders often feel powerless to change the organization's culture or its road rules. They often get frustrated trying or they learn to navigate them more effectively. Knowing the rules of the road as they pertain to actualizing your career declaration is critical. Learning the road rules for career success in your organization can be achieved by asking two simple questions:

- What do people get in trouble for around here?

- What do people get rewarded for around here?

These should be asked of multiple people inside your group, outside your group, and especially in the departments in which you want to shape your role. You also want to ask different types of people—those who are new, people with lots of tenure, those who are successful, and those who are struggling. As you ask these questions, listen to the commonalities and to the stories they tell from their own experience. Don't judge whether the person or the company is right or wrong, but instead remind yourself that people and organizations are inherently and necessarily nonrational. It is to be expected.

Learning what you can expect to be rewarded for and punished for in your organization is essential if you are new. Even if you are highly tenured in your part of the organization, it is worthwhile to ask these questions, as you are bound to be at least reminded of some important rules you had forgotten—and maybe learn some new ones. Clarity around the road rules in your organization will be immensely helpful in moving forward in whatever lane you choose to be in—fast, medium, slow, or the off-ramp.

The power of knowing the road rules is illustrated by someone we will call Jack.

JACK

Jack had been at his large financial services firm for five years. The company had been good to him, sponsoring him as he received his Series Six and Series Seven certifications and providing reasonable annual salary increases. In uncovering his passionate core and forming his career declaration it became clear to Jack that he wanted to move outside his customer contact role to a formal management role.

Due to his tenure in the firm, Jack felt he knew a lot about the company and didn't know if there was anything to be gained from asking about what got people rewarded or punished. However, he finally decided there might be something to learn and over the course of a week spent time asking seven people in his firm these questions. The people included his manager, his HR representative, three colleagues at his level— two who were successful and one who was struggling—a person who had been with the firm for twelve years, and a person who had been with the firm six months. These people had strong opinions, and although there were some differences, there were many similarities as well. Some of the things he heard were not new to Jack, but others were. Jack had forgotten some of the rules of the road, one especially that was pervasive and that he might inadvertently break in his quest to become a leader: Always be seen as a loyal member of the firm willing to delay personal and career desires if need be; trust that the firm will take care of those who wait.

Jack could have been frustrated by this rule of the road, feeling that he did not want to trust anything as nebulous as a firm as he anxiously embarked on bringing his career declaration to life. But instead, he realized that it was an understandable road rule, one that had probably stalled a lot of overly aggressive career "steamrollers" in the past. He decided to shape his role within the confines of this rule and move forward in a way that was not too aggressive. And Jack was able to navigate the road rules within his firm as he assumed progressively larger management roles.

In other cases people have chosen not to follow the road rules they have discovered. Such was the case with a human resources executive in the computer industry we will call David.

DAVID

David had been with his company for just under a year but was already frustrated. He had things he wanted to get done, even an agenda of his own that he had not been able to put forward. It took a lot of self-reflection, but he went through the steps to uncover his passionate core and develop a career declaration. Through this process, he realized that he needed to be driving change, to be a person who steps up and leads change in an organization. He felt it was his mission in life. To that end, David reframed his current role as one of "change agent."

When David took the step of asking various people in his organization what was rewarded and what was punished there, he gathered a lot of excellent information and stories. It was clear that one of the rules of the road was not to disagree with the most senior leadership. It seemed that executives expected compliance and punished those who disagreed too strongly and too often. David felt this rule had to be changed if this company he cared about was going to meet the challenges of the marketplace and truly elicit the best thinking in implementing the strategy.

In his quest to be a change agent, David had broken this unwritten rule of the road and assertively surfaced issues and questions to the senior leadership on a fairly regular basis. At times he experienced some backlash for this, but it didn't derail David as he was anticipating some negative response, especially from the most senior leaders. Most important, he had the stamina to drive change because he had aligned with his passion and career declaration to promote change within the company. David was aligned with what he loves, and his ideas found footing in the organization.

The examples of Jack and David illustrate two different responses you can have to your organization's road rules. You can choose to work within the rules as Jack did, or you can choose to work outside the rules as David did. Both are legitimate choices as long as they are based on a clear understanding of the trade-offs and repercussions.

Review the example below to help prepare for completing Discovery Exercise 17, which follows.

EXAMPLE
The Road Rules in Your Organization

Important road rules that are common across the organization:

- **Make the numbers.** Those seen as being responsible for the organization's not achieving a top-line or bottom-line target get in big trouble. In contrast, those who consistently make the numbers under sometimes difficult circumstances are hailed as heroes.

(cont'd)

The Road Rules in Your Organization

Important road rules that are common across the organization:

- **Be nice.** People find open disagreement distasteful. We are expected to be civil and nice to each other and resist any desire to be overtly confrontational.
- **Speed is important.** People in the organization pride themselves on the fast pace and how quickly things get done. Taking time to study something before making a decision is looked down on.
- **Relationships are really important.** People need and expect to know co-workers quite well on a personal level. Similarly, hiring decisions are made more on a person's personality and personal characteristics than on his or her relevant background for a role.

Unique road rules in the sales organization:

- **Group unity is important.** The levels of management are close-knit and protective of one another. They will cover each other's back if someone criticizes a teammate.
- **Sales leaders and employees play together.** They expect partners and employees to participate actively in lots of after-work activities. Sporting events such as golf games are especially important.
- **Debate is good.** If you are presenting and nobody is talking, you have lost them.
- **Don't be viewed as someone from "Corporate."** Programs imposed from the corporate level are looked at with distrust.

The Road Rules in Your Organization

Directions: In the space provided, record what you have learned about the road rules that exist within your organization.

Important road rules that are common across the organization:

-
-
-
-
-
-

Unique road rules in your part of the organization:

-
-
-
-
-
-

SUMMARY

- All organizations have written and unwritten rules. These rules of the road are pervasive and ingrained.

- You need to uncover and navigate the road rules in your organization—specifically the rules that propel and limit people in doing what they love.

- To uncover the road rules in your organization, and the area you want to work in, ask a variety of people the following questions:

  - What do people get in trouble for around here?

  - What do people get rewarded for around here?

- Once the rules are uncovered, you can choose when to follow them and when to ignore them, while understanding the trade-offs and repercussions.

Practice 5
Network

It's not just what you know and want,
it's who knows and wants you.
—Anonymous

Networks are established connections between people, places, and things. Computer systems, alumni associations, multilevel marketing organizations, the Internet, and even spiderwebs are types of networks. As in the natural world, establishing and using networks is critical to career survival and success.

Even with the speed, ease of access, and global reach of information, people still make decisions based on personal experience and relationships. It's in our DNA; we want to know and feel good about the people we work and partner with. Especially when making personnel decisions, people will rely on their own experiences with a person and the references of those they trust more than objective data or outstanding resumes. The "old boy" network is real—especially in countries and industries with less regulation, and where relatively few people own, manage, and enjoy ready access to wealth. This is because in environments with few legal guidelines, people will naturally form and rely on a network of relationships. Your challenge is to take advantage of this situation by getting connected and expanding your network.

In practice 5 you will learn how to extend your network to mobilize and sustain your career declaration.

Six Degrees of Separation

You've probably heard about the phenomenon known as "six degrees of separation." If you were to randomly select someone in the phone book and then investigate whether you know people who know this person, within six connections (and often fewer), you would find a trail of people who would connect you to this person. There is a whole science on networking theory that continues to refine the number of other connections that it takes before the whole world is connected. Whether it's the number of relay points via e-mail required to reach anyone in the world or the number of people who share or hear a particular message as it floats through an expanded network of relationships, it continues to reinforce how close and interconnected we all are.

The bottom line: Because relationships are ever more important to us, networks are increasingly pervasive and powerful. If you learn to develop and leverage relationships, you will establish a network that will be a constant source of intelligence and opportunity. And as you expand your network, it will increase your opportunities exponentially. The key is letting people already in your social circle know about your career declaration and continually reaching out and building new connections.

Starting with Who You Know

You learned in the chapter on step 4 that when you share your career declaration with people in your life, you begin to mobilize a network dedicated to helping you engage in your life's work. Even if your current associations don't have anything to offer in your desired career direction, within your network there are likely numerous people and resources that could be very useful to you—and you to them.

The power of networks can be seen in the various opportunities received and provided to others. Recently Joe helped an unemployed friend find a job as a financial analyst, a relative find an important prospect for a service she was selling, and a friend who is a new consultant find a potential client. In each of these cases, he did not personally give the person a job, sales prospect, or consulting assignment; he simply connected them with people in need of their services. On other days, it's not so one-sided: Joe is the one receiving opportunities through associates in his network. "What goes around comes around."

Over time your level of service will come back to you in other ways. If you start by reaching out regularly, you will be surprised at the connections and opportunities you can surface for each other. Again, the catalyst for making new connections through old acquaintances is the energy and focus of your career declaration. When they hear and feel it, they will want to help you.

Expanding to Other Networks

Another interesting thing about people networks is that they tend to be tight. If you have a longtime network of family members, friends, and associates, you probably all know each other. Making one good connection outside your current circle can connect you to a whole new network of people. As you establish more than a few of these unique connections, your network not only grows larger, it brings in very different people, ideas, and opportunities. Indeed, having a broad and flowing network is a form of intelligence.

How to Network

Having a broad network is important, but it does require you to perform active *networking*. However, we need to dispel one notion you may have about networking. You could be thinking of the stereotypical salesperson or politician constantly smiling, posturing, and going out of his way to get something from someone else. Although this may work for some, most people (the coauthors included) feel uncomfortable with this overt form of networking. We are most effective and comfortable when we can be ourselves. You have your own way of meeting new people, and as you align around your passionate core and your career declaration, your energy will attract more people and relationships.

Here are some basic techniques for building your network:

- Build your Rolodex

- Keep in touch

- Get involved in groups and associations

- Find the decision makers

- Collocate

We encourage you to review each of those techniques as described below and consider if and how it could broaden your network.

Build Your Rolodex

The proliferation of the standard business card has made it easy to quickly connect with, and keep in mind, people and what they do. When you meet people at work, in an airport, on a bus, at a party, or in a meeting, ask for their card. If they don't have a card, ask for their contact information. Even if a person's work and background seem totally unrelated to yours, you never know when you may be able to connect that person with someone else. Similarly, give your business card out freely and encourage people to contact you.

Time and again a casual meeting with the exchange of a card has led to fruitful interactions. For example, years ago on a flight from Philadelphia to Houston, Joe sat by a man we will call Cam.

CAM AND JOE _____

Cam and his family were moving to Houston, where Cam was beginning a job as a quality engineer for a diaper manufac-

turer. Even though Cam and Joe were in totally different pro-
fessions, they have kept in touch and been able to help each
other connect to people and resources they otherwise would
not have been able to access. Among other things, Joe has
received good financial advice from Cam, who later followed
his passion and became a financial advisor. Joe's wife has
helped Cam and his family obtain a favorable mortgage, sup-
porting her passion for constructing unique mortgage financ-
ing solutions, and they all enjoy personal friendship and sup-
port. All this began with a simple exchange of business cards
with someone Joe had a nice conversation with during a flight.
This and other similar experiences have taught us to keep in
contact with people we have a good experience with, even if
our career paths don't appear to cross immediately. Build this
sort of network both inside and outside your company.

Keep In Touch

It seems like all of us get so caught up in the daily challenges that
we rarely take time to reach out and contact anyone other than
immediate associates and family. The few people who make it a
priority to regularly reach out to a larger group of people enjoy the
true benefits of a robust network.

Such was the case for someone we will call Lowell.

LOWELL

Every day Lowell would make it a priority to contact someone
outside his daily set of interactions, often people he barely
knew. He would write notes of appreciation, phone people to
see how they were doing, or drop by a friend's house while in
the neighborhood. People were genuinely touched by his ges-
tures. It seemed like everyone in the city was no more than one
connection away from Lowell. This constant dialogue with
people, often people much different from himself, gave Lowell
fresh perspectives and ideas, which he applied to his passion
for real estate development and housing design. And it helped
him sell a lot of homes.

Get Involved in Groups and Associations

There are other people doing what you committed to do in your career declaration, or at least something very similar. These people likely form a relatively small network of both formal and informal associations.

Formal networks of people exist in all conceivable professions. Your country, state, or province has associations for everything from accountants to Zamboni drivers. Investigate and join an association or two that are aligned with your career declaration. Your involvement within these formal networks can connect you to people and information, opening up a wider array of promising opportunities.

Find the Decision Makers

Just as in a tight family network it is usually one person, the mother or father, who makes the big decisions, relatively few leaders make the big decisions in company networks—including disbursement of rewards. Similarly, in broader, more informal, networks only a few people have substantial influence on what is supported and completed. These people may or may not have a formal title, but people within the network always know who they are.

Even in broad global networks there are few people who make the decisions. Think of the handful of people who made high-tech venture capital decisions in Silicon Valley during the dot-com boom or the small, relatively unknown nucleus of people who finance and shape the news seen in all network, cable, and print media. Networks of people may be large, but the number of true decision makers within each is relatively small. Identifying and meeting the people inside and outside your organization who can help direct and support your life's work will result in exceptional opportunities. In practice 2, "Be the Players," we outlined a unique method for effectively influencing these critical stakeholders.

Collocate

Networks of people rely on social interaction, so even in this age of mass communication we are still most connected with the people we see in person regularly. Within a work area we tend to talk to, eat lunch with, and associate most with those people within a two-minute walk of our work area. On a macro scale, business districts are built to facilitate networking, and whole industries will often be located in the same area of the world, often with competing companies in the same hometown. That is the case with the "Big Three" American automakers in Detroit.

You need to take advantage of collocation in pursuing your life's work. Within your company, try to locate your work area near those who are also doing your life's work. This will put you in their stream of ideas and issues. You may even need to move physically to another building, city, or region. Just as aspiring actors move to Los Angeles and country musicians to Nashville, you may need to move to a "corridor of competence"—the place where the people with similar career passions meet, support each other, and make decisions.

Building Your Network

Applying the networking approaches above can increase your connections and opportunities, but don't treat them as simply "check-the-box" steps for finding opportunities. If you don't enjoy doing an activity and don't see how it will directly support the achievement of your life's work, then it will likely be a waste of your time. Focusing on the activities that energize you, rather than some formula for networking, will catalyze others. Digest these techniques, think of them some more, and then deploy the ones that work for you.

Study the example of how one person prepared notes for building his network, as you prepare to complete Discovery Exercise 18, which follows.

EXAMPLE
Building Your Network

- **Build your Rolodex.** I will order new business cards that list my name and the type of work I am passionate about. I will look for opportunities to exchange these business cards and will keep detailed track of contacts on my PDA.

- **Keep in touch.** I will make a list of people whom I could reach out to but generally don't. Every day I will contact one, even if it's a short e-mail message.

- **Get involved in groups and associations.** I will research the local quality, Six Sigma, and process improvement associations in my area to find one that has an emphasis on the specialty area of sales and service functions. I will join and network with the people in this specialty area.

- **Find the decision makers.** I will talk to the Six Sigma people I know inside my company to find out how things really work: Who decides which people become Black Belts? Who chooses which projects will be worked on by a Black Belt? Once I have identified the key decision makers, I will meet with them and share my intentions and career declaration.

- **Collocate.** I will spend more time with the Six Sigma people in the company. I will invite them to lunch and see if I can find an office in their area.

Overall:

I will continue to tell people about the work I am passionate about as described in my career declaration.

DISCOVERY EXERCISE 18
Building Your Network

Directions: Record your own declared intentions for building your network under each of the following techniques:

• **Build your Rolodex.**

• **Keep in touch.**

• **Get involved in groups and associations.**

• **Find the decision makers.**

• **Collocate.**

Overall:

SUMMARY

- Networks are established connections between people, places, and things.

- As illustrated by the "six degrees of separation," we are all close and interconnected.

- Begin a network—connect with people you already know.

- Expand your network—meet new people and tap into their networks.

- Five techniques for building your network include the following:
  - Build your Rolodex
  - Keep in touch
  - Get involved in groups and associations
  - Find the decision makers
  - Collocate

- Don't wait—go forth and build your network . . .

Practice 6
Check In

Your vision will become clear only when you look into your heart.
. . . Who looks outside, dreams. Who looks inside, awakens.
—*Carl Jung*

In practice 6 you will learn how to stay connected with the source of your career success—your heart.

Checking in refers to the practice of self-assessment to ensure you're staying centered. We begin the discussion of this practice with the story of Maureen (not her real name), who loved acting and helping people to learn and grow.

MAUREEN

Acting and helping people to learn and grow were Maureen's purest expression of her passionate core needs. Based on these passions, Maureen found a role as a corporate trainer, a perfect role for her, as she was able to use drama to teach and train. Her classes were always highly rated, as she made each class a work of art, each with more impact than the last. She used creative skits and role-plays to make mundane topics such as safety and compliance entertaining and informative.

After three years in her role, Maureen had achieved about every formal and informal form of recognition the organization had to offer. In her annual performance review she was consistently rated outstanding and received high merit increases and regular cash spot awards. More important, she was doing what she loved, and she and the organization were in a mutually value-adding relationship.

At about this time Maureen's manager decided to retire, leaving this leadership role open. A number of people were interviewed for the position, including Maureen. Given her stellar performance, Maureen felt she should be the top candidate for the role. However, the vice president of training chose someone from outside the organization instead. In discussing this issue with the new vice president she agreed that the role of a manager would take her away from her passionate core needs, but she felt she should have been at least offered the position and had the choice to turn down the role first. The vice president of training and other key leaders in the organization tried to assure Maureen that she was still valued by the organization. However, Maureen's pride was hurt, and she left the role and organization she loved for another company. At the time of this writing Maureen was making her new role work, but she was not as fulfilled as she had been and she longed for the passion she had in her old role before she was "betrayed" by her old company.

Who is at fault for Maureen's departure? In some ways everyone, and in some ways nobody. Everyone was acting in good faith and with integrity. As is so often the case, however, here passions turned into success, and then turned sour. People might hear this, shrug, and say, "Good things can't last forever," but there's more to it than that.

With success come recognition, financial reward, and heightened expectations. It's only human to get used to the accolades and cash, but it can be dangerous. Subconsciously we may begin to embrace the accolades and money, and a sense of pride and comfort with the external symbols of success may replace the pure joy and fulfillment derived from doing what we love. In the case of Maureen, these symbols of success had become so important that she was willing to walk away from what she loved and had built. The work she loved had not changed. What had changed was Maureen's expectation and desire for the money and special handling from the board of directors. It's really too bad that these extraneous things got in the way of Maureen doing what she loved. They would not have gotten in the way had she followed the critical practice of *checking in*—staying centered on what she loved and not letting all the other "noise" distract her.

Good Things Can Last

Yes, good things *can* last when it comes to doing what you love. But it requires checking in on a regular basis—that is, deliberately evaluating why you are doing your work—ensuring that you still love the content of your work and that you are not tied to symbols of success such as money, titles, or recognition. If you have not achieved these symbols of success, you may spend your time lusting after them. If you have achieved them, you may spend your time trying to protect them. If either is true, the initial passion that propelled you will not continue to drive your success because your heart is focused on what you lust for, not on what you love. You have limited what you are and could bring by muzzling the intelligence and artistry of your heart.

We've referred to a number of successful people throughout the book. And we have illustrated how consistently the root of their success is their passion for the work they do. Their work is at the heart of who they are. It's not a job; it's their passion. Their work sustains them and results in a career of health and success. For each person we have cited, there are many more who started with a pure love of their work but along the way got enticed by money, titles, and recognition and lost touch with what they loved. They may have experienced a short period of exhilaration but it led to a long road of mediocrity and even disappointment.

Like the many "one-hit wonders" in popular music and professional sports, many people in organizations have had flashes of
brilliance coming from the heart. Think about the people you work
with every day who talk about the "good times" or back when they
excelled. In many cases they didn't continue to excel because they
got sidetracked. Probably without even realizing it, they gave up
what they love to "get ahead." Ironically, it's the few people who
stay focused on what they love to do who find sustained career
success, while those who focus on doing what is expected to get
ahead, disregarding their passionate core needs, have a career of
mediocrity. It leads us to this universal conclusion: As soon as the
pure love for your work is replaced by lusts and desires, you ensure
that your good things will not last.

Resisting the desires that can derail you and staying focused
on what you love is a simple principle, but it is not always easy,
especially initially. At times it requires you to do things that seem
irrational, causing others to question your actions. For example, it
seemed irrational for Michael Dell to quit school to start a computer company and for Carly Fiorina to drop out of law school with
no other career plans or options to fall back on. Those who find
career wealth and success ultimately follow their heart, not their
head.

At other times your personal sense of right and wrong or your
temporal desires and pride may cause you to make choices that are
not aligned with your heart. You may take a job you are not passionate about because it pays more money, or you may feel you
have to leave a role you love because you don't like your manager.
These are examples of socially justifiable reasons for making
career choices that have the unfortunate effect of distancing you
from your heart while sentencing you to less career wealth and
success at the same time.

Staying Plugged In

Essentially, checking in is the process of continually keeping
plugged into the source of your career energy and success, your
heart. An excellent tool for measuring the level of alignment with
your heart is the Career Wealth Indicator you completed in chapter 1. Return to this instrument periodically, as it will tell you how

heart-centered your work is at any given time. Then ask yourself the questions below. They will help you to resolve the issues that will inevitably pop up and possibly cause you to move away from your core needs and loves.

✓ **"Why am I working?"** In answering this question, go through all possible reasons for getting up and going to work every day. Be honest with yourself: Decide whether a desire for money, fear of your manager, or the allure of a more prestigious title has replaced the simple satisfaction of doing what you love. Ask yourself slightly altered versions of the two questions you answered earlier:

- If you knew you had five years left before you die, would you continue in your current role and work?

- If you were independently wealthy, would you continue doing your current work?

If you didn't answer yes to both questions, you are likely out of alignment. If this is the case, be careful not to rationalize the lack of alignment by thinking that the short-term pain and misalignment is a necessary step in your progression to a career of doing what you love. Clearly, at the beginning there may be some transition and even sacrifice before you are fully doing what you love. However, if your progress is stalled, you may need to get on a totally different track soon. Remember career truth #16 from the second chapter: Paying your dues truly is a waste of time.

✓ **"Does my career declaration still energize me?"** Career creators and shapers must be flexible. Just because you have chosen a path and are following the practices in "Career Navigation"—the outer band of the Career Wealth Model—to achieve it does not mean you are wed to these activities.

Real career creators know that written declarations are simply documents. They provide guidance and direction only, and as such are flexible and subject to change or modification. Remember, your declarations and career navigation practices should serve what you want, not the other way around. Remain flexible. If you gain a deeper understanding of what you love, you may want to modify your career declaration and the career navigation activities for achieving it. These adjustments are totally okay if they lead to greater alignment with your heart and are not motivated simply by a desire to take an easier path.

✓ **"How am I developing?"** Bringing your career into alignment with your heart takes work. In fact it is a major part of your life's work. It really doesn't matter what stage of development you are in—wherever you start, you should be getting better. And it is this development that you should be assessing. As authors, we ask ourselves every day, "Are we getting better at writing, thinking openly, and helping others to bring their loves into their work?" Simply put, as we get better in these areas, we will have more opportunities to do these things we love. The same is true for you.

Whatever you have chosen to do in your career, whether it be engineering, managing, marketing, building houses, playing the guitar, or some other pursuit, you should be a lifelong learner, always getting better within your chosen path. Regularly assess your development; give yourself a grade on your progress and get feedback from others.

✓ **"Do I believe my own press?"** Developmental feedback is critical. But while it's important to have people help you get better, try to filter out the career advice noise that will likely come your way. People and their opinions can be the biggest reason for career derailment. At times it will be tempting to give up what you love to get along with, and be accepted by, people around you. Doing so, however, has the dangerous effect of having you focus on people's respect and affirmation instead of what you love to do. Making choices based on what people think of you at any one moment creates a shaky foundation on which to build a career because their subjective opinions will change and you will be left to constantly change with them. Seek feedback for the purpose of getting better at your life's work, not to be popular and accepted.

Not believing your own press is especially important when you find success. We have seen many leaders and professionals become imperious after a year or two of success. They start believing what people are saying about them, thinking that they are as smart as others think, and really enjoying the adulation. In fact, much of their effort turns to maintaining and obtaining more adulation. With more money than they really need, they become adulation junkies, living for the spotlight. In the process, they stop listening and stop learning. Ultimately this leads to their downfall and a lot of pain for the people and organizations around them. They could avoid all this by staying motivated by what they love to do, regularly seeking to improve themselves instead of spending their time and effort shaping what they want others to think about them.

The bottom line of the practice of checking in is this: Heart matters all the time and in every stage of your career. If you remember this simple fact, you *will* realize a career doing what you love.

SUMMARY

- Stay plugged into your heart—it is the source of your loves, energy, and passion.

- Critical to checking in to keep your career heart-centered is asking yourself these questions:

  - "Why am I working?"

  - "Does my career declaration still energize me?"

  - "How am I developing?"

  - "Do I believe my own press?"

Epilogue

Your
Commencement

Life is a process of becoming, a combination of states we have to go through. Where people fail is that they wish to elect a state and remain in it. This is a kind of death.
—*Anaïs Nin*

At the beginning of the book, we discussed the pervasiveness of organizations in our lives. For most of us, the organizations or companies in which we work have a significant impact on our happiness and quality of life. However, organizations are not in the business of accommodating our loves and needs. In fact there are subtle but strong forces in organizations that can distance us from what we love and need. The good news is this: You don't have to wait for your organization to change to find greater passion and fulfillment in your career. You can take control of your career and your life now within your current organization. Helping you do this has been the main objective of this book.

Do the Work

It will take some time to complete the steps, practices, and corresponding exercises in this book if they are going to have full impact on your career and life. The process requires you to thoughtfully consider and apply each of the principles. If you have reached this point and have not established your career foundation and planned how you will apply the six practices of career navigation, then this book will not yet have succeeded in propelling you down the path to career wealth and success.

Not yet. Many of us need to understand the whole picture or process before we can jump in and complete the steps. If this is true for you and at this point you have simply read the book, go back now and do the work. Complete the Career Wealth Indicator. Review the sixteen career myths and internalize the sixteen career truths. Uncover your passionate core, isolate career choices, and finalize your career declaration. Then apply the practices in "Career Navigation," the outer band of the Career Wealth Model, to ensure that the organization in which you have chosen to work constantly supports you as you do what you love.

Begin Your Commencement

Graduation ceremonies represent the end of your years in school and the commencement, or beginning, of a new chapter in your life. Similarly, completing the work of *Make It Work* represents your commencement of a career and life marked by greater love, passion, and fulfillment.

As authors we spent years uncovering and exploring the concepts outlined in this book before we realized the full power of their application. When we finally went from a cerebral understanding of these principles to a deep choice to bring our passionate core into our careers, we realized exponentially higher levels of passion and fulfillment. So, please, go from thinking to doing—commence your transformation.

Let's Stay Connected

In creating *Make It Work* we have shared a piece of our heart with you. We really do want to keep in contact with you. Fortunately, with modern technology it is relatively easy to reach out to support and learn from each other. Please take the time to visit our website: www.careerswork.com. Let us know what you think and feel. And if you wish, tell us your story. Feel free to send us an e-mail—we will make every attempt to reply.

Our best to you in navigating your career without leaving your organization.

Joe Frodsham   Bill Gargiulo

Index